THE USBORNE
RAINY
DAY
BOOK

THE USBORNE
RAINY
DAY
BOOK

Edited by Alastair Smith
Designed by Fiona Brown

Material in this book originally developed by
Heather Amery, Anne Civardi, Marit Claridge, Ray Gibson,
Rebecca Heddle, Judy Hindley, Susan Mayes, Kate Needham,
Clare Rosen, Alastair Smith, Louisa Somerville,
Judy Tatchell, Falcon Travis, Jenny Tyler,
Mike Unwin, Carol Varley, Gaby Waters,
Angela Wilkes, Kate Woodward,
Caroline Young

Illustrated by
Simone Abel, Fiona Brown, Stephen Cartwright,
Kate Davies, Malcolm English, Colin King,
David Mostyn, Graham Potts, Graham Round,
Angie Sage, John Shackell, Guy Smith,
Sue Stitt, Lily Whitlock,
Nadine Wickenden

First published in 1994 by Usborne Publishing Ltd, Usborne House, 83-85 Saffron Hill, London, EC1N 8RT, England.
Copyright © Usborne Publishing Ltd, 1994, 1992, 1991, 1990, 1989, 1987, 1985, 1984, 1983, 1977, 1975.
The name Usborne and the device ♔ are Trade Marks of Usborne Publishing Ltd.
Printed in Spain.
UE First published in America March 1995.

Contents

DRAWING, PRINTING AND PAINTING

You don't have to be an expert to make really good drawings and paintings. You don't even need to limit yourself to using the usual artist's tools. For instance, you can create works of art that include blobs of paint blown through a straw. You can also make monsters by painting with the side of your hand. These techniques, and others, are shown on the following pages.

⚠️

To avoid harming yourself take extra care wherever you see a red warning triangle.

Hand prints

Using a bit of imagination and following the simple ideas shown on these pages you can come up with some amazing looking creatures and plants. You might want to put them together to create a scene.

Munching monster

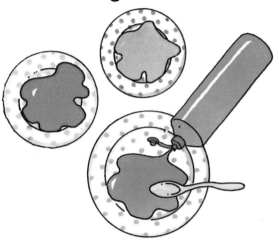

The more shapes you make like this, the bigger your monster's body will be.

1. Put about five teaspoonfuls of paint onto each plate or lid. Spread the paints around with the teaspoon, until they cover most of the plates.

2. Clench your hand into a fist and press it into the paint. Rock your hand from side to side making sure it is well coated with paint.

3. Press the side of your fist onto a sheet of paper, then lift it off. To make the body, put more paint on your hand and repeat the prints in a line.

Draw the horns using a finger dipped in paint.

Using white paint, add thumbprints for the eyes. Print the middle parts using black paint on your fingertips.

Print the front of the middle part of your fingers to make the monster's head.

Print petals like these with your thumb, and the flower's middle with a fingertip.

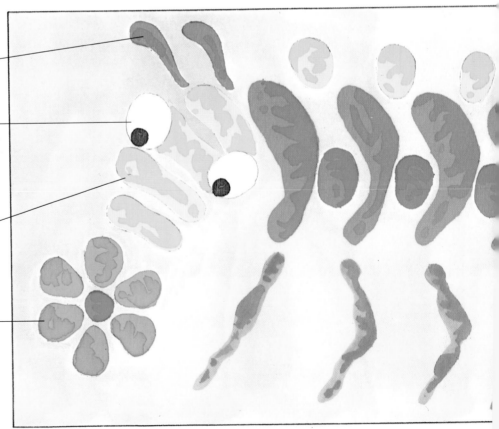

Alternative subjects

Bees on flowers

On yellow paper, use the front of your bent fingers to print the black bodies of bees. Allow the bodies to dry and add white thumbprint wings. Add the antennae, using a paintbrush. Print some big bright flowers.

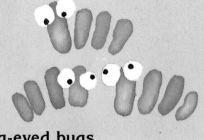

Big-eyed bugs

Print the bodies with the front of your clenched fingers, and the eyes using your fingertips. You could use the prints to make birthday cards.

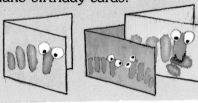

Spot and wipe dragonflies

Press a paint-covered fingertip onto some paper. Pull the paint into a tail and then lift it off quickly. Add some wings with the side of your little finger and draw in the antennae.

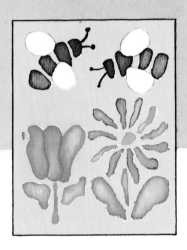

You could create your own monsters based on real creatures such as fish or birds, if you want.

Q. How do you scare a monster?

A. Tell it that it doesn't really exist.

Print extra details on the creature's body using your fingers and thumbs.

Q. What time is it if you meet a hungry monster?

A. Time to run.

Printing tips
- Before you start, print different parts of your hand to try out the various shapes that you could make.
- Change hands to make prints curve in the opposite direction.
- Wash your hands before you use a different paint.

To taper the tail, finger print it, starting with your thumb and finishing with your little finger.

For spindly legs, print using the side of your little finger.

Printing with blocks

With printing blocks you can use a decorative design over and over to create an eye-catching pattern. When you have printed a shape, wipe the shape clean before you use another shade of paint, or the next print might look dull. When you design a shape, remember that it will be the other way around when you print it.

Q. What has stripes and sixteen wheels?

A. A tiger on roller skates.

Q. What's the definition of a slug?

A. A homeless snail.

String block prints

1. Start by drawing a simple shape or pattern onto a block of wood. Try to draw it without taking your pen off the block, so that the shape is made of one continuous line. You could add a few lines around the main shape, for emphasis.

2. Cover the block with glue. Put the string onto the pattern that you have made, then leave the glue to dry. When it is dry, scrape off any loose glue from the string and block, using a blunt knife.

3. Pour poster paint onto a tray or plate and spread it out evenly. Place the block onto the paint. Make sure that the shapes that you want to print are covered with an even layer of paint.

4. Lay down several sheets of newspaper, then put a sheet of plain paper on top. Place your paint-covered design onto the paper. Press firmly and evenly on the block to make a good print.

Printing tips

- Try out your printing blocks by making test prints. That way you can be sure that you like the design before you print anything permanent.

- To make professional looking prints, plan the pattern that you'd like to make before you start printing.

Cardboard prints

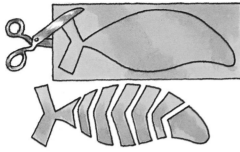

Choose where you want the shapes to go before you place them on the block.

1. Draw a shape, smaller than the block of wood, on a piece of thick cardboard. Next, cut out the shape, either in one piece or in several pieces, as shown here.

2. Spread glue over the wooden block. Arrange the shapes on top of the glue and press them down. Let the glue dry before starting to print with the block.

Striped prints

Print using the thick cardboard first.

Print with corrugated cardboard second.

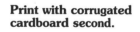

1. Cut an outline shape out of thick cardboard and glue it to a block of wood. Dip the shape into thick, bright paint and use it to make as many prints as you need.

2. Cut the same shape out of some corrugated cardboard and glue the flat side to another block of wood. Dip it in a dark paint and press it over the first prints.

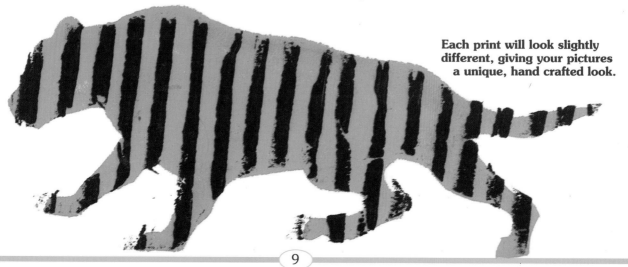

Each print will look slightly different, giving your pictures a unique, hand crafted look.

Dinosaur stencil

The striking shapes of dinosaurs make them ideal for turning into stylized pictures. Start with a simplified sketch, then make a stencil and use it to create lots of impressive effects.

You will need
• Thin cardboard
30 x 20cm (12 x 8in)
• Scissors • Pencils
• Piece of candle • Paints
• Old toothbrush
• Old plates, or
lids from containers
such as jam jars
• Chalks • Crayons

Making the stencil

To begin, sketch the dinosaur's shape onto some thin cardboard. The simpler the shape you draw, the easier it will be to cut out.

Carefully cut out the shape so that you can use both the positive and negative stencils. For the best results, use small, sharp scissors.

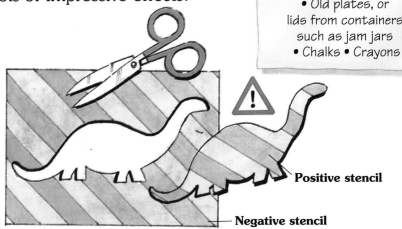

Positive stencil

Negative stencil

Candle wax textures

1. Place the negative stencil over some paper. Paint through the hole with yellow. Use the paint sparingly or it will seep under the stencil.

2. When the paint is dry, take a thin candle and use it to draw wrinkles and scaly patterns over the dinosaur. The candle will resist any more paint you use.

3. After you have finished with the candle, keep the stencil in place and paint the dinosaur shape with a layer of dark blue-green.

Making the background

When the dinosaur shape is dry, cover it with the positive stencil to protect it. Then paint the sun first. When the sun is dry, cover it with candle wax and add swirls and lines of wax for clouds. Paint over the top with pink fading to yellow. Then add plants, water and reflections.

Paint plant silhouettes in a pale mauve. When dry, draw on stem and leaf shapes using candle wax, then add dark mauve on top.

To make the effects of reflections, apply wiggly lines of wax before adding the paint.

Spatter painting

Using the negative stencil, some paint and a toothbrush, you can make pictures that look like the one shown here. To begin, mix different shades of paint on old plates or on the lids from old containers. Then lay down the negative stencil and apply a layer of pale green paint. Leave this to dry. Dip a toothbrush into a darker mix of paint. Draw the edge of your finger or a ruler back across the bristles, allowing the paint to flick onto the dinosaur's shape.

The paint flicked from the toothbrush makes a spatter effect.

Add more spatters at the bottom, to create a darker area, which looks like it is in shadow.

Q. Which fierce prehistoric creature could fly and run, breathed heavily in its sleep and lived in Texas?

A. The Fly-run-o-snore-us Tex.

Scratch out the eye and mouth shapes with a pin.

Chalk and crayon

To turn your dinosaur around, reverse your stencil. The one below has been decorated using crayons. You don't need to give the dinosaur hard outlines. Instead, make it look rounded by adding crayon lines in curves.

Use the side of some chalk to make bold block shapes on the background. To stop the chalk from smudging you should apply a light covering of fixing spray when you have finished drawing. You can buy fixing spray from most art shops.

Add the eyes and the mouth last, using a dark pencil.

Curve the lines around the body shape to make it look rounded.

Q. What do you call a dead, smelly dinosaur?

A. Ex-stink.

Make the body shape look solid by criss-crossing the lines, using your crayon.

Cartoon people

Compared to real people, cartoon people have simple body shapes. By varying the basic shapes of their bodies and faces you can come up with lots of different looking characters. Once you have mastered the technique you can go on to draw your people in different poses and situations.

Q. What vegetable do artists fear most?

A. Arty-chokes.

Basic figures

Use a pencil, so that you can erase the lines later.

Body

Keep this line short or the figure will look bottom heavy.

Erase part of the head line here, where the hair falls forward.

1. Using a pencil, draw a stick figure, just like the one shown above. To ensure a funny result, make sure that the head is large, but not larger than the body.

2. Here are the outlines of some clothes for the figure. You could copy these onto your sketch. Alternatively, design other clothes, such as a dress or dungarees.

3. To dress your stick figure, draw the clothes around it, starting at the neck and working down. You could add any type of hair that you like, such as long and straight or short and curly.

Hands and feet

When someone is facing you, you can see their thumbs and first fingers, as shown here.

People's feet usually turn out a little, as shown here.

Like cartoon heads, cartoon hands and feet are larger than on a real person. You might like to try drawing these shapes on their own before you add them to your figures.

Decorating your cartoons

Use a fine felt-tip to make an outline.

A cartoon person's head is larger than on a real person.

Erase your sketched pencil lines when you've finished drawing your characters.

White patches emphasize the shine on the shoes.

When you have finished drawing the outline in pencil, go over it with a felt-tip pen. When the felt-tip is dry, erase the pencil marks. Decorate the rest of the cartoon brightly.

To make bare legs draw a straight line down each side of the stick leg lines. You can add socks if you like, as shown in the picture of the girl, above.

Rounded sketch shapes

Make sure that the arms are a bit shorter than the body, but the legs are longer.

Smoothed-off join

These stripes are slightly curved to show the rounded shape of the body.

1. Using a pencil, draw a head shape. Add an oval for the body shape and sausages for the arms and legs. The body is about one and a half times as long as the head.

2. Add the outlines of the clothes, smoothing off any joins, such as between the arms or legs and the body. Go over the outline using a pen, then erase the pencil lines.

3. Add hands and feet and then decorate the clothes with bright felt-tips, paints or crayons. If you show stripes on the clothes curve them slightly, to show the rounded shape of the body.

More cartoon people to draw

The pictures below show some of the different looking characters that you can draw by varying a cartoon's basic sketch shapes.

Q. Where do you bury a dead cartoon character?

A. In a car-tomb.

This tall person has an egg-shaped head and longer body.

Tiny person. The head is large in proportion to the size of the body.

This short person of average build has the same length head, body and legs.

Fat person. The head is wide compared with its height and the legs are short.

Improve your technique

To improve your drawing technique, try sketching the characters described on the right, or invent your own.

• A fat lady with hair tied back, wearing an eye-catching red ball gown and a sparkling diamond necklace.

• A friendly man, with short spiky hair, wearing a raincoat, straight dark trousers and big brown boots.

Scratch pictures

Using a selection of wax crayons and the techniques shown on these pages you can make vivid scratch pictures. For the most striking effects use bold designs.

Paint-on-wax picture

See the steps below to find out how to make a picture like the one shown here.

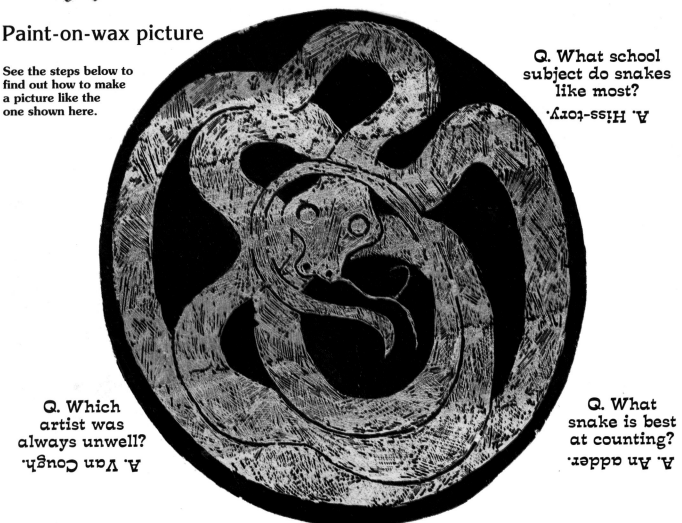

Q. What school subject do snakes like most?

A. Hiss-tory.

Q. Which artist was always unwell?

A. Van Cough.

Q. What snake is best at counting?

A. An adder.

1. Using a selection of wax crayons, draw several wide bands onto a piece of white paper. Press down hard on the crayons so that you make the bands look strong.

2. Paint over all of the lines using black poster paint or drawing ink. If the wax lines are difficult to cover, brush on two or three thick coats.

3. When the paint is dry, scratch your design into it using the handle of a paintbrush. This will show the wax beneath. You could leave parts untouched, to add to the stylized effect.

Wax-on-paint picture

On this picture, the scratched shapes complement the monster's jagged features.

Black paint or ink

Wax shapes

Scratch out the patterns.

1. Paint a shape on a sheet of white paper using black poster paint or black drawing ink. The shape that you choose to paint will form the outline of your picture.

2. When the paint is dry, draw patterns all over the black shape using a selection of wax crayons. Press hard on the crayons, making bright, bold, shapes.

3. Use a paintbrush handle to scratch through the crayon, to reveal black beneath the wax. Make the scratching haphazard, to emphasize that the picture has been made by hand.

Space collage

A collage is a picture that is made by sticking things, such as pieces of paper, onto a background. The word collage (pronounced koll-large) comes from the French word *coller*, meaning "to stick". This one includes planets that you make by printing paint bubbles onto pieces of paper.

Q. Where do aliens park their spaceships?

A. On a parking meteor.

1. Dot the piece of black paper with white paint to make a starry sky. Then put it to one side until it is dry.

2. To make bubble prints, start by mixing some paint with half a cup of water, so that it is fairly runny.

3. Add a squirt of dishwashing liquid to the paint. Stir it well with a teaspoon until it is completely mixed in.

Don't suck the straw, or you'll get a mouthful of paint.

4. Place the straw in the mug and blow until the bubbles rise above the rim. You could stir the straw around in the paint to make more bubbles.

Don't leave the paper on the mug for too long or the bubbles might smudge.

5. Lay a piece of paper over the bubbles gently. Then lift off the paper without dragging it. Allow the paint to dry on the piece of paper.

6. To make planets, cut out the bubble prints using scissors. You could draw around bottle tops to make smaller planets, asteroids and moons.

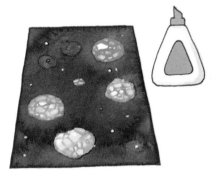

7. Glue the planets onto the starry background. Vary their sizes to give the scene lots of impact.

Other ideas

You could experiment with the type of paper and the shades of paint that you use.

Print one paint on top of another for an unusual effect.

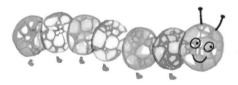

Overlap cut-out bubble prints to make a long caterpillar. Glue the shape onto paper, then paint its eyes and feet.

Additional ideas

You could use these drawings of an alien and a spaceship in your space bubble collage. Paint them with vivid shades to create a strong effect. Alternatively, you could decorate them with various coverings, such as reflective cooking foil on the spaceship or old cloth on the alien.

You can make meteors by dipping your thumb into paint and pressing it onto the paper.

Add comets by pressing paint from your finger onto the paper, then wiping it across the paper in a curve.

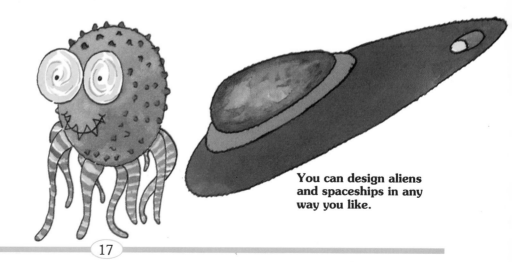

You can design aliens and spaceships in any way you like.

Witch's tree

Trees with long, twisted branches and no leaves can look creepy, especially at night. By blowing paint through a straw, you could paint your own creepy tree. By adding other things on and around the tree you could make a scene like the one below.

Q. Why is it difficult to identify witches?

A. Because you can never tell which witch is which.

⚠️
Remember, don't suck through the straw, or you might get a mouthful of revolting paint.

1. Mix blue paint with some water so that it is runny. Dip a damp sponge into the paint and then squeeze it gently. Wipe the sponge across white paper several times.

Make sure that the background is completely dry before you begin painting the scene. If it is not dry, any further painting will sink into the paper, giving a smudged effect.

2. Pour some large blobs of runny black paint near the middle of the paper. Join the blobs and make a tree shape by blowing hard through a straw. Allow the paint to dry.

3. Paint and cut out a witch, along with her belongings and a moon, then glue them onto your picture. Mount the picture on a piece of black paper. Your end result could look like the picture on the left.

Other ideas

By blowing paint through a straw you can make a variety of different scenes. For example, you could make a bright green jungle tree with creepers. Add thumbprint leaves and glue on painted animals and flowers.

You could add animals to your jungle scene, such as toucans, parrots and monkeys.

THINGS TO MAKE

The following projects show you how to make a selection of useful and attractive things. For example, you can learn how to print wallpaper, make mobiles featuring bees and snails and create brilliant pop-up birthday cards. You won't need much experience to come up with good results – but you will need a little time to complete the projects.

⚠️

To avoid injury take extra care whenever you see a red warning triangle next to an instruction.

Mobiles

Mobiles are good for brightening up your room. They are especially effective if you place them above your bed, so that you can see them when you are lying down.

You will need
• Sheet of red paper • Sheet of blue paper • White paper
• Black felt-tip pen • Pencil
• Ruler • Glue • Scissors
• Thin wooden sticks • Thread

Bees

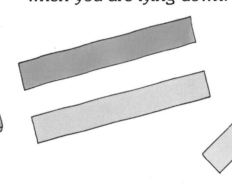

You could use any shade of paper you like to make your bees.

1. Line up a ruler along the edge of a piece of paper. Draw a line along its length, about 4cm (1½in) from the side.

2. Cut along the line to make strips. Next, using the red paper, make identical strips to the ones you just made in blue.

3. Glue the two strips together at one end, at right angles. Let the glue dry before you go on to the next stage.

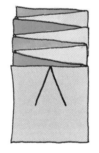

4. Bend the bottom strip over the top strip and press firmly. Repeat this stage until all the paper has been used up. Glue the last piece down firmly.

5. Cut an upside-down V shape into an end piece. The V should end at about the middle of the square of paper. Bend the piece down to make a nose.

6. To make two wings and two eyes, copy the shapes shown above, onto a piece of paper that has been folded in two. Then cut them out.

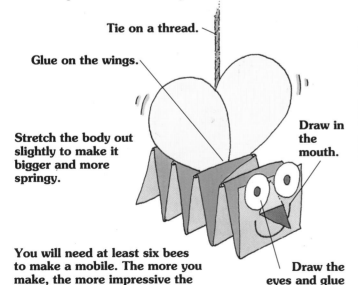

Tie on a thread.

Glue on the wings.

Stretch the body out slightly to make it bigger and more springy.

Draw in the mouth.

You will need at least six bees to make a mobile. The more you make, the more impressive the end result will be.

Draw the eyes and glue them on the face.

Assembling the mobile

Tie thin wooden sticks of different lengths together. Plant support sticks are ideal. Make sure that each stick is balanced before you secure it.

Q. What goes zzub-zzub?

A. A bee flying backwards.

Snails

Like the bees on the opposite page, the snails for this mobile can be made from just a few strips of paper. After you have learned how to put the basic snail shape together, you could make smaller and larger ones, to give more variety to your mobiles. Also, you could use various patterns and shades of paper, to make the snails as eye-catching as possible.

Q. What do snails use to make their shells shine?

A. Snail polish.

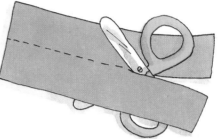

1. To begin, measure and cut a rectangle from the original piece of paper. It should measure about 16 x 3cm (6½ x 1in).

2. Fold the paper in half, long edge to long edge. Then press along the fold, to ensure that you make a sharp crease.

3. Open the paper and cut along the crease to make two equal strips of paper. Make the cuts as straight as possible.

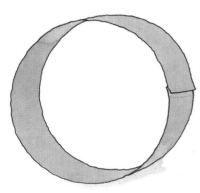

For variety, you could give your snails different expressions

4. Spread a small amount of glue on the end of a strip. Then bend the paper over and glue the other end to it, to make a complete circle.

5. To create some horns for the snail, cut a small square out of the other strip. Draw the eyes and a mouth, using a black felt-tip pen.

6. Turn the strip over and spread glue in the middle. To save glue, don't spread it up to the edge of the strip.

Press the circle and strip together firmly to secure them.

Making the mobile

Make several snails and use thread to hang them from a stick as shown.

Balance the stick by sliding it left or right through the middle loop. When it is balanced, tie it firmly in place.

You could make a mobile with both bees and snails on it.

A ring at the top will help the mobile twist and turn.

Thread

Stick

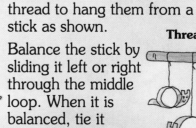

7. Attach the circle to the glued section of the second strip. Lift up the head so that it sticks up around the circle.

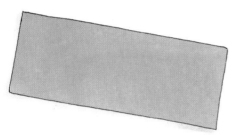

Decorations

Paper decorations are ideal to put up when you celebrate a party or festive occasion, or even if you just want to brighten up a room. The lanterns on this page look like traditional Chinese lanterns.

Chinese lanterns

For more variety, make your lanterns from a selection of different papers.

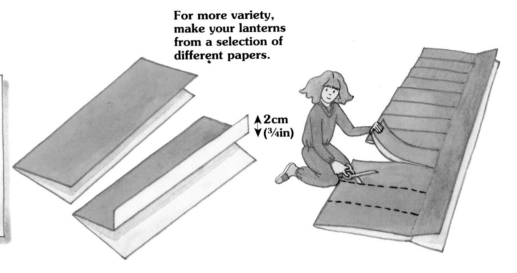

You will need
(for each lantern)
- Bright, eye-catching paper 15 x 25cm (6 x 10in)
- Glue
- Adhesive tape
- Scissors
- Cotton thread

2cm (¾in)

1. With the paper's plain side facing you, fold it in half along its length. Make folds 2cm (¾in) from the long edges as shown above.

2. Open out the 2cm (¾in) folds. Cut strips about 2cm (¾in) wide as shown by the dotted lines in the picture above, as far as the fold.

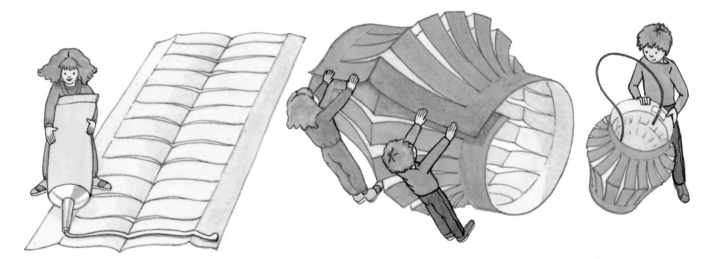

3. Open the paper so that its plain side is facing you again. Spread a small amount of glue all the way along one of the end strips.

4. Bend the paper into a tube and press the two end strips together. Ensure that the paper is stuck together, and will not come apart later.

5. Using adhesive tape, loop a length of thread across the top of the lantern. This way, you will be able to hang it up wherever you like.

Streamers

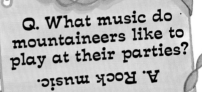

Cut into strips.

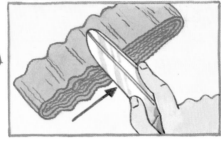

You will need

- At least one packet of crêpe paper
- Adhesive tape
- Scissors

1. Cut the crêpe paper into strips 5cm (2in) wide. Then run the outside of the scissors down both edges of the strips, as in the top picture. This will make the paper wrinkle.

2. When you have wrinkled all of the paper, unwind the strips and join them together with adhesive tape. Twist the streamers and attach them to the ceiling.

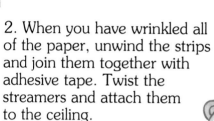

Decorated balloons

You will need

- Bright, eye-catching paper
- Balloons
- Glue
- Scissors
- Felt-tip pens
- String

1. To begin, blow up the balloons. Then cut a variety of shapes or faces out of paper and decorate them with felt-tip pens. If your decorations are for a special event, you could make the shapes suit the theme of the event.

2. Choose decorations that are best suited to each balloon. Put a dab of glue on each shape, then attach them to the balloons. Tie a piece of string to each balloon, so that you can fix them to walls and doors.

If you are going to have a party, make sure that you have enough balloons to give one to each of your guests as they leave.

Pop-up cards

You can give people pleasant surprises by sending them cards that pop up when they are opened. To make the two examples shown here you will need to trace the templates shown on page 93. When you are used to the techniques, you could adapt the basic shapes and make cards that have other things popping out of them, such as birds or submarines.

You will need

- Thin black cardboard
  12 x 24cm (4½ x 9in)
- Tracing paper
- Pencil
- Blue cardboard
  15 x 25cm (6 x 10in)
- Blue cardboard
  20 x 30cm (8 x 12in)
- Paper • Glue
- Pencil crayons

Bat and moon

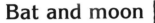

Fold line

1. Fold the black cardboard in half across its length. Trace the bat template onto it, using a pencil. Trace the fold line on the wing of the template.

2. Cut out the bat. Fold the wings along the fold lines, first one way, then the other. This will make them lie easily in your finished card.

3. Open out the bat. Make sure that the middle fold stands up slightly. The folds in the wings should point down, in the opposite way to the middle fold.

4. Turn the bat over. Put glue between the wing-tips and the wing folds, as shown above. Turn it over again.

5. Position the bat inside the smaller piece of blue cardboard. Press the glued wings inside the card, so that the middle of the bat lies in the fold.

6. Close the card gently, pulling the middle fold of the bat to you. Press all over the card.

7. Cut out a moon shape. Glue the shape on the card so that the bat is in front of it.

Finishing touches

To complete the card, add a church, a tree or some stars to the background.

Try making the card in different shades, for different effects.

Rocket

This rocket card is folded and glued in the same way as the bat and moon card. However, its lively subject matter makes it look less sinister and more wacky than the last project.

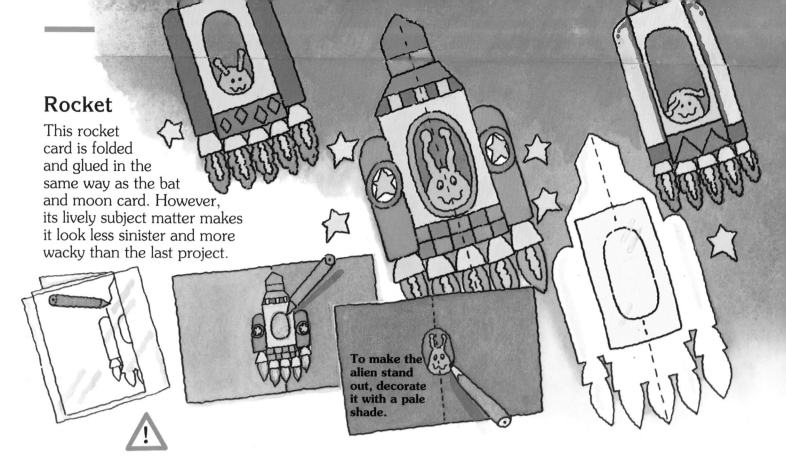

To make the alien stand out, decorate it with a pale shade.

1. Trace the template onto folded white paper. Cut around the outline, then cut out the window. Decorate the rocket with bright pencil crayons.

2. Fold the blue cardboard in half along its longer side. Lay the rocket in the middle. Draw around the window onto the cardboard beneath.

3. Draw an alien about 4.5cm (1¾in) long on some paper to fit in the window shape. Decorate it, cut it out and glue it inside the window shape on the blue cardboard.

4. Cut a piece of tracing paper 3.5 x 7cm (1½ x 3in). Glue it onto the back of your rocket shape, to make glass for the window.

Q. What do you get if you cross a tennis court with a space vehicle?
A. A tennis rocket.

Q. What do you call a chicken from outer space?
A. An ali-hen.

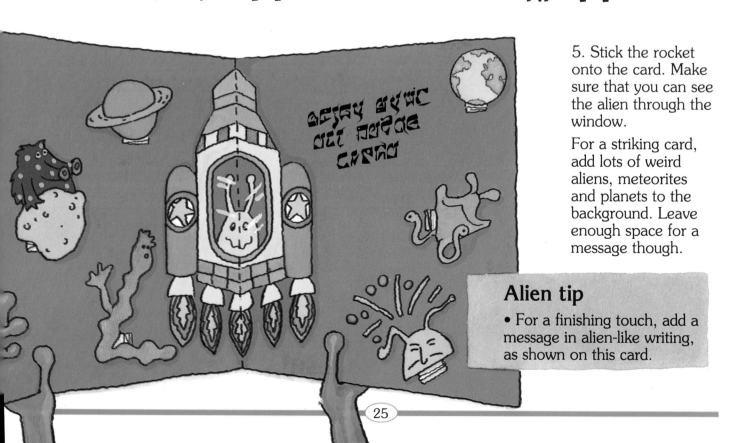

5. Stick the rocket onto the card. Make sure that you can see the alien through the window.

For a striking card, add lots of weird aliens, meteorites and planets to the background. Leave enough space for a message though.

Alien tip

• For a finishing touch, add a message in alien-like writing, as shown on this card.

Wallpaper print

Using the methods shown on these pages, you can make repeated patterns. You could use these to print striking posters, which you could use to decorate your room. Use a large piece of drawing paper, or the back of some used computer paper to print on.

An old cooking foil box is ideal for this job.

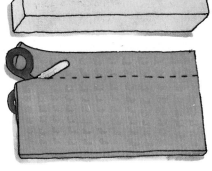

1. Close the lid of the long narrow box. Use adhesive tape to seal the lid and to cover sharp edges, if there are any.

2. Using the long side of the box, measure a strip of thin sponge. Then cut off the strip, using scissors.

3. Snip the strip into shapes such as rectangles and triangles of various sizes. Save the leftover pieces.

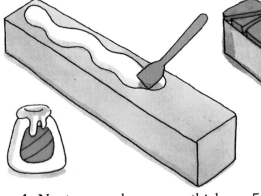

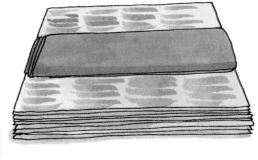

4. Next, spread an even, thick layer of glue along the top of the box. Go on to the next stage before the glue dries.

5. Press your sponge shapes into the glue. Use small leftover pieces in the gaps. Allow the glue to dry.

6. Fold a piece of cloth so that it is a little longer and wider than the box. Place the cloth on a thick pad of newspaper.

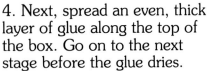

Printing tips

- Instead of using sponge, you could print with types of cloth, such as corduroy or felt.

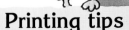

- You could print using vegetables cut in half, or cut simple shapes into a halved potato.

- Also, try printing with pasta, pencil ends, crushed paper, coiled model dough, corrugated cardboard and leaves.

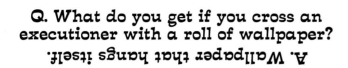

Q. What do you get if you cross an executioner with a roll of wallpaper?

A. Wallpaper that hangs itself.

More printing tips
- Test your design by printing it onto some scrap paper, to see if you like it.
- Fold sponge shapes in half, then snip out the middles, using scissors.

7. Moisten the cloth with a little water. Apply the paint as shown above and spread it evenly with the back of a spoon.

8. Press the box firmly into the paint. Rock it from side to side in the paint to cover the sponges evenly.

9. Firmly press the box onto some paper. To make a clean print, lift it off carefully. Don't drag it across your paper.

10. Continue to make prints down the length of the paper. To vary the pattern, turn the box around after every few prints that you make.

Other ideas

You could print a border on a paper tablecloth.

Print on tissue paper to make wrapping paper.

Decorate the inside of a box with prints to make a miniature room.

Use two or more boxes to create a collection of different prints.

Use different shades of paint to create varied results.

Printing letters

You can make letters for printing using a whole range of materials, using things such as cork, vegetables and bits of cardboard. When you have made enough letters you could use them to print signs and posters. You could even use them to print slogans on old T-shirts (but check that you may do this before you start).

You will need
- Sharp knife • Pencil
- Mirror • Paints
- Paintbrush
- Old plate • Glue
- Various materials to print letters from, such as potato, cork, polystyrene, string, cardboard, corrugated cardboard, or paper

Making a printing block

1. Begin by cutting the block so that it has a flat surface. You'll have to use a sharp knife, so be careful.

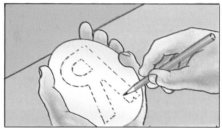

2. Using a pencil, draw a reversed letter onto the block's surface so that it will print the right way around.

3. Take the block and check it in a mirror to make sure that the letter is right before you cut it out.

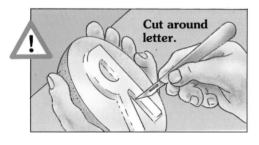

Cut around letter.

4. Using a pointed knife, carve around the letter so that its shape is raised up. Cut out any spaces within the letter, too.

Press down firmly.

5. Next, brush some paint or ink onto a flat plate. Press the printing block onto the paint to cover the surface of the letter.

6. Finally, press the block firmly onto the paper. Make sure the block does not slip sideways as this will smudge the letter.

Creating texture

Printing blocks made from different materials can create unusual effects. You could experiment using a variety of different textures, as with the examples on the right. You might also like to use different thicknesses of paint, to see how they affect the texture of your prints.

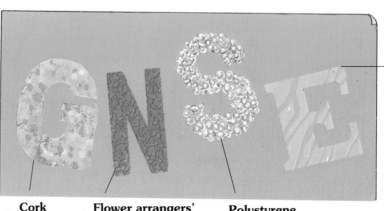

Scratches give a cracked effect.

Cork

Flower arrangers' foam, called oasis.

Polystyrene

More printing blocks

You can make a printing block by gluing a letter shape onto a piece of wood. The surface has to be flat and the letter needs to be made out of something raised, such as string or a piece of corrugated cardboard. Before you cut or glue your designs, don't forget to check them in a mirror, to make sure that they are correct.

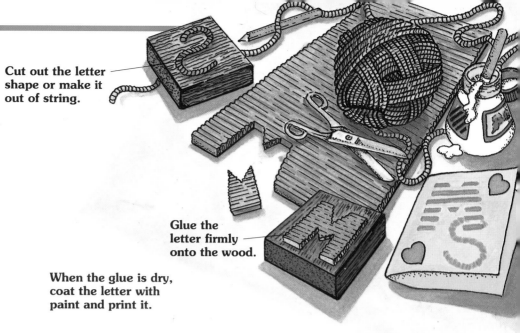

Cut out the letter shape or make it out of string.

Glue the letter firmly onto the wood.

When the glue is dry, coat the letter with paint and print it.

Printed letter designs

By repeating letter shapes you can form intricate patterns and pictures, similar to the ones shown here. For a regular looking design, use letters with lots of straight edges, such as the letters F, E, L and T. For a more wiggly pattern, use curled letters such as S, C or Q.

Q. Why did the woman cut out the alphabet and put it in an envelope?

A. Because she liked to send letters.

Famous monograms

Designs made out of letters are called monograms. Companies sometimes create monograms from their initials so that people will remember their names. Here are some famous monograms. You could try making a design out of your own initials.

Coco
Chanel

Volkswagen

Rolls
Royce

Letter shapes

You can avoid cutting out every letter by making blocks for basic letter shapes. Below are the four shapes you will need.

You can combine the shapes upside down and both ways around to make the letters. This method is useful for creating longer messages.

Basic letter shapes

Piggy bank

This piggy bank is made by gluing layers of wet paper around an orange. It must be made over the space of a couple of days, in order to allow the paper to dry before you decorate it. For a bigger piggy, use a large grapefruit instead of an orange.

Q. Where do pigs leave their cars?
A. In a porking space.

You will need

- An orange
- 4 sheets of newspaper
- Glue or wallpaper paste
- Adhesive tape
- 4 toothpaste tops
- Cork • Scissors
- Knife • Paint
- Varnish (clear nail polish works well)

This technique is called papier mâché, which is French for "mashed paper".

Q. Where do beavers keep their money?
A. In a river bank.

1. Tear the newspaper into lots of small pieces. Put the pieces into a bowl of water and soak them for a few minutes.

2. Press a layer of paper around the orange. Spread wallpaper paste or glue over the paper, then press on more paper.

You should repeat stage 2 five or six times.

3. Put the orange somewhere warm overnight. When the paper is dry cut all around the orange neatly and carefully. Then take out the orange.

4. Along the edge of one half of the paper ball, cut a slot big enough to accept a large coin. Then put the halves back together, using adhesive tape.

5. Cover the ball with two more layers of paper. Use the edges of the newspaper that have no print on them so that the ball is completely white.

Papier mâché tips

• Don't soak your paper for too long or it will turn to pulp.

• Mix your wallpaper paste so that it is fairly stiff. This way it will dry quicker than if it is very runny.

• To speed up the drying process, you could use a hair dryer to dry out the papier mâché.

6. Glue the toothpaste tops onto the bottom of the orange to make legs. Cut off the end of a cork with a knife and glue it onto the front to make a snout.

7. You could cut a hole in between the legs so that you can get the coins out. Plug the hole with a cork, so that the money doesn't fall out.

8. Put another layer of glue and paper all over the pig, covering its legs and nose.

9. Paint the pig with thick paint. When it is dry, paint a face and a tail. Allow the paint to dry, then varnish the piggy bank to make it shine.

Octopus tablecloth

A paper tablecloth printed with simple pictures can make a great scene that will brighten up any meal time. To complete the theme, print paper cups and napkins with sea creatures, and use them at the same time. Before you begin printing, lay your tablecloth on a flat surface, with old newspaper under it.

You will need

- Paints • Newspaper
- Old plates
- Drinking straw
- Pieces of thick cloth
- Old spoon
- Old fork • Knife
- Black felt-tip pen
- Round, white self-adhesive labels
- Two or three different kinds of vegetables such as potatoes, carrots and sprouts
- White (or pale) paper tablecloth

Printing pads

1. Begin by placing a piece of thick cotton cloth on an old plate. Pour on a good quantity of paint.

2. Spread the paint evenly over the pad using the back of a spoon. Make one pad for each paint that you will use.

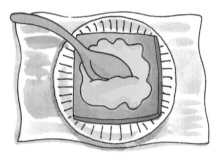

While printing, protect your clothes by wearing overalls.

3. With your fingers spread, press one of your hands onto the printing pad. Press firmly onto the tablecloth.

Boulders

Cut a potato in half. Score the cut surface by drawing the prongs of a fork firmly across it. Overlap the boulders when you print them, if you like.

When an octopus shape is dry, add self-adhesive labels for the eyes and draw pupils with black felt-tip pen.

You could overlap your boulders, as shown here.

Printing tips

• To cover your hand in paint, press it firmly on your printing block and rock it to and fro.

• Print onto an old plain cotton cloth if you have one, using textile paints. For the best results, make sure that you follow the instructions on the paints' packs.

Other ideas

You could print octopuses onto paper cups. Mix the paint with glue to make it waterproof.

Print giant flowers using halved apples for the middles. Use hand prints for the petals.

Little fish

To make fish, use your thumb to print the bodies. Make tails using the end of your forefinger. Make eyes and mouths with a felt-tip pen. For the bubbles, print with the end of a fat drinking straw.

Q. What are cold and squeeky?

A. Mice-icles.

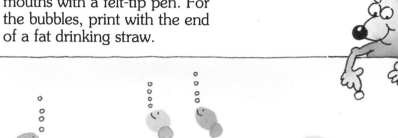

Press the side of your hand into the paint and print with it, to make seaweed shapes.

To make shapes like these, you could use a Brussels sprout, cut from top to bottom.

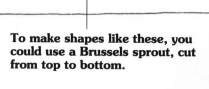

Print slices of carrot for shells.

Striped shells

Cut the end off a fat carrot. Slice the carrot in half, as shown, and then cut slanting stripes. ⚠️

To make a handle to hold the carrot, push a fork into the back. Wash and dry the carrot before you use it with a different shade of paint, so that the shades do not mix and give a dirty effect.

You could print striped caterpillars, using the carrots that you used to make shells. Use self-adhesive labels to make the eyes. Print the underside of large leaves for a background.

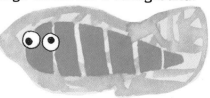

This striped caterpillar was printed in the same way as the striped shells. Adhesive labels with dots drawn onto them have been added to create eyes.

Desk tidy

You can make desk tidies from just a few cardboard tubes and matchboxes. They make good presents, especially for grown-ups who are disorganized.

You will need

• 3 tubes from kitchen or lavatory paper • 2 large sheets of wrapping paper • Cardboard 20 x 15cm (8 x 6in) • Bread knife • 4 empty matchboxes • Scissors • Glue • 4 paper fasteners

The pen holder

1. Using a bread knife, cut the tubes into three lengths. Cut out pieces of wrapping paper big enough to go around each, with a little left over.

2. Wrap a piece of paper around each tube. Glue the edges together and fold in the overlap at each end. Make sure that your wrapping is tidy.

3. For the base, lay the cardboard on some wrapping paper. Draw around it and cut out the paper. Glue it onto the cardboard to make the base.

Tidy trays

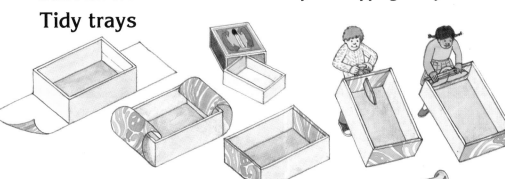

4. Take the trays out of the matchboxes. Cut four strips of paper the same width and twice as long as the trays. Wrap them around the trays and glue them on.

5. Push a paper fastener through the middle of one end of each tray. Bend back the arms on the inside of the drawer.

6. Glue the four matchboxes together, as shown above. Cut out a piece of paper long enough to go around them all.

7. Glue on the paper all the way around. Trim off the edges. Glue the matchbox onto a corner of the base.

8. Glue around one end of each tube and stick them onto the base. Stick them together where they touch.

CREATIVE COOKING

The delicious recipes in this section include a variety of snacks, main meals and desserts. You can also find out how to make typical American and Italian food.

All of the ingredients are cheap and should be easy to get at your local supermarket, but you may find that you have them at home already.

⚠

Take care when you are cooking as even the best chefs sometimes burn themselves. To warn you, a red triangle appears wherever part of a recipe could be dangerous.

Hot food

Always wash your hands before you make any food. Also, make sure that the things you use to make the food, such as bowls, knives and saucepans, are properly clean.

Surprise baked tomatoes

You will need

- 4 large tomatoes
- 4 eggs
- Salt and pepper
- 1 tablespoon chopped parsley, if you have some
- Ovenproof baking dish
- Spoon
- Sharp knife

Oven setting: 180°C (350°F)

For this recipe, use the biggest tomatoes you can find.

1. Before you prepare the food, grease a shallow, ovenproof baking dish and set the oven to the correct temperature.

2. Cut a small slice off the top of each tomato and scoop out the pulp with a spoon. Season inside the tomatoes.

3. Put the tomatoes in the dish and break an egg into each one. Season the eggs and sprinkle parsley on top.

4. Put the tops on the tomatoes and bake them in the oven for about 20 minutes until the eggs have set.

5. Eat the tomatoes while they are hot. They are delicious if you eat them with lots of crusty bread and butter.

Welsh rarebit

Welsh rarebit was originally called "Welsh rabbit", although nobody is sure how the food got its name. It is a simple dish to prepare, consisting mostly of toasted bread, with melted cheese on top. You can add various seasonings to the cheese, to make it even more delicious. As examples, try using dried herbs, pickles, ketchup or pepper.

You will need

- 4 slices of bread
- 125g (1½cups) grated cheese
- 1 beaten egg
- 1 teaspoon of mustard
- Sliced tomatoes
- Dash of Worcester sauce
- Salt and pepper
- Mixing bowl
- Knife

Cooking heat: high

Q. What's purple and fixes pipes?

A. A plum-er.

1. Mix the cheese, egg, salt and pepper, mustard and Worcester sauce together in a bowl.

2. Toast the bread lightly, on one side only. Don't let it burn, or you will spoil the taste.

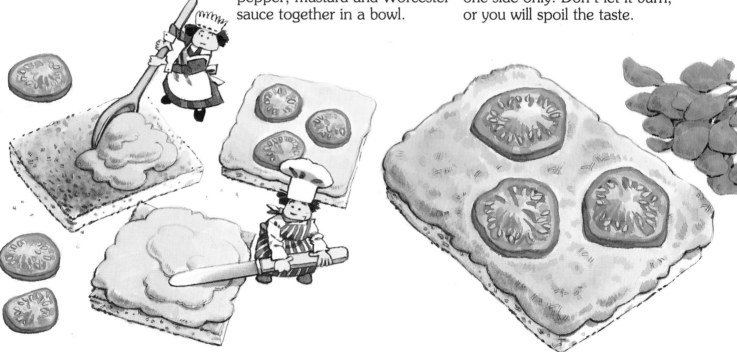

3. Spread the cheese mixture thickly over the untoasted sides of the bread and put the sliced tomato on top.

Q. What kind of mouse can eat the most cheese?

A. One with an enormouse appetite.

4. Put the toast back under the heat until the cheese is bubbly and light brown. Put it on a warm plate and eat it right away.

American cooking

For many years, people from all over the world have chosen to go and live in the USA. Because of this, American cooking has lots of different styles, which started in the countries where the people lived originally. For example, hamburgers were first made in Germany.

Q. What food do vampires like best?

A. Leeches and scream.

Pancakes

Traditional American pancakes are fairly small and thick. They are sometimes called flapjacks. They are good for breakfast, with bacon and eggs or with sweet maple syrup. The recipe shown here makes about ten pancakes, which should be enough for two people.

You will need

- 150g (1 cup) plain flour • 2 teaspoons baking powder
- Pinch of salt • 1 egg • 300ml (1 cup) milk
- 3 tablespoons vegetable oil
- Maple syrup (or a substitute such as golden syrup or warmed jam)
- Frying pan • Strainer • 2 mixing bowls

Cooking heat: medium

1. Sift the flour, baking powder and salt into a medium-sized mixing bowl.

2. In another bowl, whisk the egg, two tablespoons of oil and all of the milk.

3. Beat this liquid into the flour. Put the mixture to one side until you are ready to cook it.

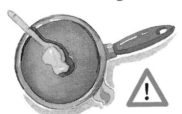

4. Put the last tablespoon of oil into a frying pan. Heat it until a faint haze rises from the pan.

5. Using a ladle or a cup, pour two or three small pools of pancake mixture into the pan.

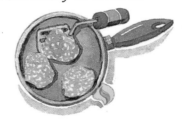

6. When the pancakes bubble, flip them over, then cook the other side.

Maple syrup

Maple syrup comes from the sap of maple trees. Each tree produces only about two bottles of syrup in a year, so it is expensive to buy.

You could serve your pancakes with jam, ice cream or any other sweet topping that you like.

Hamburgers

The first hamburgers were made in Hamburg, Germany. German settlers probably first took the recipe to America, but American cooks have made hamburgers famous around the world. You can cook them in almost any way that you like, with delicious results.

You will need

- 500g (1lb) lean hamburger meat
- 1 small onion, chopped • 4 soft buns
- 2 tomatoes • 4 lettuce leaves
- Pinch of salt and pepper
- Mixing bowl • Vegetable oil
- Frying pan or grill/broiler

Cooking heat: hot

1. Put the meat, onion, salt and pepper into a mixing bowl. Gently squeeze them into a ball with your fingers.

2. Divide this ball into four. Pat each portion into a burger shape 1cm (½in) thick and the same size across as your buns.

3. Divide the buns into two flat halves. Toast the insides until they are lightly browned, then lay them out on a plate.

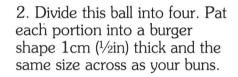

4. Put oil on both sides of the burgers, using a pastry brush or a kitchen towel. This will keep the meat from burning.

5. Cook the burgers for about five minutes on each side. If you fry them, cook them in a shallow pool of vegetable oil.

6. While the burgers cook, wash the lettuce and tomatoes and dry them. Then slice up the tomatoes.

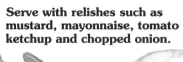

Serve with relishes such as mustard, mayonnaise, tomato ketchup and chopped onion.

7. Put a lettuce leaf, some tomato and a burger onto the bottom half of each bun. Put the top half onto the filling and then press gently.

Banana milkshake

Milkshakes go well with hamburgers. Here's how to make a fresh banana milkshake for one person.

You will need

- 300ml (1 cup) milk
- 1 chopped banana
- 1 scoop of vanilla ice cream
- Blender or whisk

Add a banana and ice cream to the milk and mix them for two minutes. Pour the mixture into a tall glass and serve with a straw.

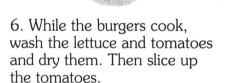

Leek and tomato soup

This soup makes an excellent meal, eaten with fresh bread and butter. It takes about an hour to prepare, so you should start making it well ahead of your meal time. If you don't want to eat it right away, let it cool and then store it in a sealed container in the refrigerator or freezer.

Q. What food do porcupines like best?

A. Spine-apples.

You will need

- 375g (¾lb) tomatoes
- 30g (1½ tablespoons) butter
- 375g (¾lb) potatoes
- 375g (¾lb) leeks
- Milk
- 2 teaspoons of sugar
- 720ml (2½ cups) water
- Salt and black pepper
- Sharp knife
- Large bowl
- Large saucepan
- Blender

Cooking heat: medium

1. Using a sharp knife, peel and dice the potatoes carefully.

2. Drop the tomatoes into some boiling water. Leave them for a minute, then lift them out.

3. It will now be easy to peel the skin off the tomatoes. Chop them up roughly, using a sharp knife, then put them to one side.

4. Cut off the leeks' tops and roots and peel the outer layer. Cut them lengthwise and rinse them in water. Chop them finely.

Q. Which superhero looks like a can of minestrone?

A. Soup-erman.

Take care not to burn the leeks when you cook them, or you'll spoil their taste.

You could keep the chopped vegetables in bowls until it is time to cook them.

5. Gently melt the butter in a big, thick-based saucepan. Add the leeks and cook them slowly until they are soft.

6. Add the chopped tomatoes. Stir them into the leeks and let them cook slowly until their juice starts to run.

7. Add the potato, salt, water and sugar. Cover the pan and simmer the soup for 20 minutes until the vegetables are soft.

8. Take the pan off the heat. To make the soup smooth, put it in a blender for a minute or so. Alternatively, you could push the solid chunks through a colander with a wooden spoon.

⚠️ Take care when tasting the soup. It might be extremely hot.

9. Pour the soup back into the pan and reheat it gently. Taste it and add more seasoning if you like.

10. Stir some milk into the soup and serve it right away.

Fun foods

The foods shown here are great fun to make. The faces shown at the bottom of the opposite page could be used as the basis for a game. Each contestant starts with the basic ingredients and tries to make the funniest face.

You will need

- 4 canned pineapple rings
- 4 slices of thinly cut ham
- 4 slices of processed cheese
- 4 small slices of bread
- Absorbent kitchen towels
- Small bowl
- Spatula
- Butter

Cooking heat: medium

Ham, cheese and pineapple slices

1. Open the can of pineapples and drain the juice into a bowl. Then pat the pineapple pieces dry using absorbent kitchen towels.

2. Using the can as a cutter, press out four circles from the bread, four circles from the ham and four circles from the cheese.

3. Toast the bread lightly on both sides. Let it cool, then spread some butter onto it on one side only.

4. Put a circle of ham onto each round of bread. Then top it with a slice of pineapple and a piece of cheese.

5. Using a spatula, place the food under the heat and cook it until the cheese is melted and bubbling.

Chef's tip

- If you have any scraps of bread left over after you have done your cooking, break them into crumbs. Then either freeze them in a plastic bag, to use on another day, or feed them to the birds.

Mini-pizzas

1. Toast some circles of bread. Spread them with tomato paste.

2. Sprinkle bits of vegetables and ham, salami or tuna on top.

3. Top with cheese and a sprinkling of herbs. Cook until the cheese bubbles.

Hedgehog nibbles

You will need

- 500g (1lb) cream cheese
- Party snacks, such as corn chips
- Carrot sticks
- Cucumber slices
- Raisins • Large plate
- Bowl • Milk
- Spoon
- Large cloth

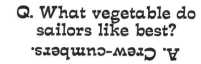

Q. What vegetable do sailors like best?

A. Crew-cumbers.

1. Before you mix the ingredients, rest the bowl on a cloth to stop it from slipping.

2. To soften the cheese, mix it with a tiny amount of milk. This will make it easier to shape.

3. Put the cheese on a plate and pat it into a pear shape with the spoon.

Use raisins to make eyes and noses.

Cucumber and cream cheese make a delicious combination.

4. To make prickles, press the raw vegetables or some other party snack into the cheese.

Bright food tips

- You can make pink hedgehogs by adding a little tomato ketchup to the cheese.

- You might like to try sweet hedgehogs, using pieces of canned or fresh fruit for prickles.

Faces

You could use a selection of sliced, shredded or chopped vegetables to make faces on bread circles, spread with butter or cheese spread. A couple of possible faces are shown here.

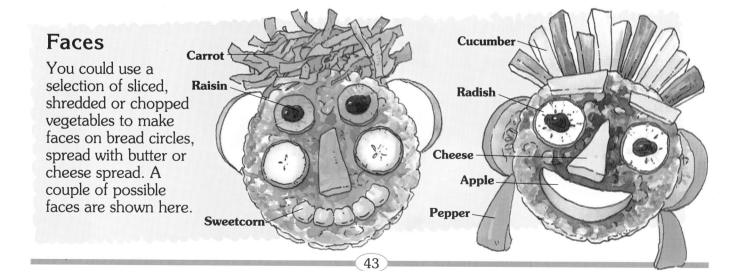

Carrot
Raisin
Sweetcorn

Cucumber
Radish
Cheese
Apple
Pepper

Italian cooking

Q. What do mushrooms use to help them count?
A. Their fungus.

Many Italian foods combine the tastes of meat, vegetables and herbs. The meals shown here are classic examples of Italian cooking. Each will take you an hour or two to prepare. They will serve two hungry people, or three if you are not so hungry.

You will need
- 250g (1½ cups) bread flour
- 1 tablespoon dried yeast
- 1 tablespoon sugar
- 150ml (½ cup) warm water
- 400g (14oz) can tomatoes
- 2 tablespoons tomato paste
- 60g (1 cup) grated cheese
- ½ teaspoon dried oregano
- Pinch of salt and black pepper
- 2 small bowls
- Large bowl
- Chopping board, with flour sprinkled on it
- Greased baking tray

Oven heat: 230°C (450°F)

Pizza Margherita

You can serve pizza hot or cold.

1. Mix the sugar and dried yeast with two tablespoons of warm water in a small bowl. Leave it in a warm place until it turns frothy.

2. Put the flour and salt into another bowl. Pour the yeast and the warm water into it. Gently squeeze the mixture into a ball.

A crisp salad goes well with pizza.

3. On a floured board, stretch the dough out, then fold it over. Press down on it with your palm. Repeat this movement over and over.

Set the oven while you wait for stage 4 to be completed.

4. When the dough is soft put it in a greased bowl. Cover it with a damp cloth and leave it in a warm place for an hour to rise.

For alternative toppings, put onions, grilled bacon bits, olives, peppers, mushrooms, sweetcorn, pineapple, or tuna onto your pizza crust.

5. Knead the risen dough a little more. On a greased baking tray, press it into a round shape about 1cm (½in) thick and 30cm (12in) wide.

6. Pour away the juice from the canned tomatoes. Chop them up in a bowl. Stir in the tomato paste, oregano, salt and black pepper.

7. Spread the tomato mixture evenly over the pizza crust. Sprinkle with grated cheese and cook for about 25 minutes, until golden on top.

Spaghetti bolognese

Bolognese sauce was first made in the city of Bologna, in northern Italy. (Bolognese is pronounced bolla-naze.)

You will need

- 500g (1lb) minced/ground beef
- 3 slices of bacon, cut into strips 2cm (1in) wide
- 1 medium onion, chopped • 1 medium carrot, chopped
- 60g (¾ cup) mushrooms, sliced • 1 clove of garlic, peeled and crushed
- 1 medium can tomatoes • 2 tablespoons tomato paste
- 90g (6 tablespoons) butter • ½ teaspoon dried oregano
- ½ teaspoon dried basil • 375g (12oz) spaghetti • Water
- Large frying pan • Large saucepan • Strainer

Cooking heat: medium

1. Melt half the butter in the frying pan. Add the bacon, garlic, onion, carrot and the mushrooms and fry them until they are soft, but not burnt.

2. Add the beef to the mixture and cook it until it browns. Then add the tomato paste, canned tomatoes, basil and oregano.

3. Add about 4 tablespoons of water and simmer the sauce for 20 minutes, with the lid on. Stir it quickly after ten minutes.

4. Boil 2l (8 cups) of water in a large saucepan. Put the spaghetti ends in, then slowly push them all in as they soften.

5. Boil the spaghetti until it is soft (it will take about eight minutes). To drain it, pour it into a strainer.

Eating spaghetti

Eating spaghetti is tricky. Try winding it around a fork. Use a spoon to stop it from slipping off the bottom.

6. Lift the spaghetti onto four plates, using two forks. It is slippery, but if you lift it quickly you are less likely to drop it. Add the rest of the butter and spoon on the sauce.

Pasta

Spaghetti is one of over 50 sorts of Italian pasta. Pasta means "dough" or "paste" in Italian. It is made from flour, eggs and salt mixed together. It should be cooked until it is soft but not soggy. Italians call this *al dente*.

Pasta sheets are called lasagne. Cooks put vegetables or meat between layers of lasagne and cheeses, with sauce on top.

These pasta tubes are called macaroni. They are often served in cheese sauce.

Pasta can be made into fancy shapes, like these.

This brown pasta has some wholewheat flour in it.

If spinach is added to pasta, it is called pasta verde (pronounced vair-day). *Verde* means "green" in Italian.

These pasta envelopes are called ravioli. They are often stuffed with meat, but they can have other fillings such as cheese and spinach.

Hard grated cheese, called Parmesan, is delicious sprinkled on spaghetti.

Q. What's tall, sweet and French?

A. The trifle tower.

Sweet treats

For these recipes you will need to bake your ingredients in a baking pan that measures about 18 x 28cm (8 x 12in). Before you start cooking, wipe a thin layer of margarine around the inside of the pan, using a clean kitchen towel.

Q. What food do builders like most?

A. Wall-nuts.

Oatmeal squares

<u>You will need</u>

- 250g (2¾ cups) oats
- 125g (½ cup) butter
- 60g (½ cup) brown sugar
- 1 tablespoon golden syrup
- 90g (½ cup) raisins
- 1 teaspoon salt
- Saucepan • Margarine
- Medium sized baking-pan

Oven setting: 180°C (350°F)

1. Begin by melting some butter in a saucepan, over a low heat. Don't let the butter burn, or you'll spoil the taste of the food that you'll cook in it.

2. With the saucepan still on the heat, add sugar and syrup to the butter. When they are mixed, take the pan off the heat and stir in oats, raisins and salt.

3. Stir everything together well, then pour the mixture into the baking pan and press it down. Bake for 20 minutes.

4. Cut the cookies into squares. When they are cool take them out of the baking pan. Store them in an airtight container.

Oatmeal squares are fairly chewy and are very filling.

Chocolate brownies

Chocolate brownies are delicious sweet treats that were invented in the USA. When they are properly cooked they have crisp tops and are really soft and rich below.

You will need

- 110g (1 cup) butter
- 110g (4 squares) dark chocolate
- 225g (1 cup) sugar
- 2 beaten eggs
- 110g (1 cup) plain flour
- ½ teaspoon baking powder
- 110g (1 cup) chopped walnuts
- Pinch of salt
- Mixing bowl • Saucepan
- Medium-sized baking pan
- Wire cooling rack

Oven setting:
180°C (350°F)

Make sure that you mix all of the ingredients thoroughly.

1. Before you begin cooking, grease the baking pan. Then heat a small saucepan of water until it is fairly hot, but not so hot that it boils.

2. Break the chocolate into a mixing bowl and add the butter. Then fit the bowl over the saucepan of warm water. Take care not to burn yourself.

3. When the butter and chocolate have melted, take the bowl off the heat and stir in all the other ingredients, using a wooden spoon.

BROWNIES ARE DELICIOUS WHEN THEY ARE BROKEN UP AND MIXED WITH ICE CREAM.

4. Spread the mixture into the baking pan. Leave it to settle for a minute or so, then bake it in the oven for 30 minutes.

5. After you have removed the cooked brownies from the oven, leave them to cool in the baking pan for 10 minutes.

6. Cut the brownies into squares. Remove them from the pan and cool them on a wire rack. Store them in an airtight container.

Frozen desserts

These cold foods will take a while to prepare because you will have to freeze them. However, they are so tasty and refreshing that they are well worth the wait. They will take about an hour to freeze, depending on how cold your freezer is.

Banana treats

1. Pour four or five tablespoons of honey into a saucer and cover a plate with some nuts.

2. Halve the bananas. Insert a clean ice-cream stick into each half banana. Holding it by the stick, brush it with honey.

3. Roll each banana in nuts until covered. Then arrange the bananas on a plate covered with clingwrap and freeze them.

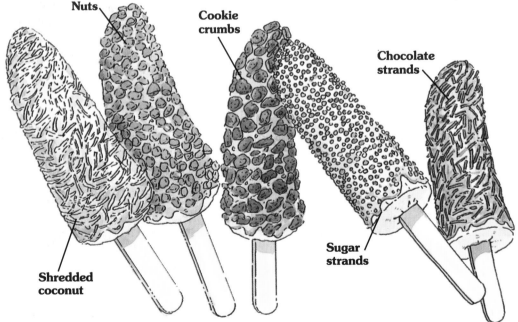

Nuts

Cookie crumbs

Chocolate strands

Sugar strands

Shredded coconut

Frozen dessert tips

- If your honey is stiff, stand the jar (without its lid) in a little hot water for a minute or so.

- Use the handles of plastic spoons if you do not have any ice-cream sticks.

- Remove frozen desserts from the freezer ten minutes before you eat them.

Yogurt melties

You will need
- 3 tablespoons frozen orange juice, unthawed • 6 tablespoons natural yogurt • Sugar to taste • 3 tablespoons water

Mix all the ingredients together until they are mashed thoroughly. Then pour them into an ice-cube tray. Freeze them and use the cubes when you need them.

Frosty fruit

For a simple dessert, freeze some fruit juice or the syrup from sweetened canned fruit. Don't forget to add ice-cream sticks before you put them in the freezer.

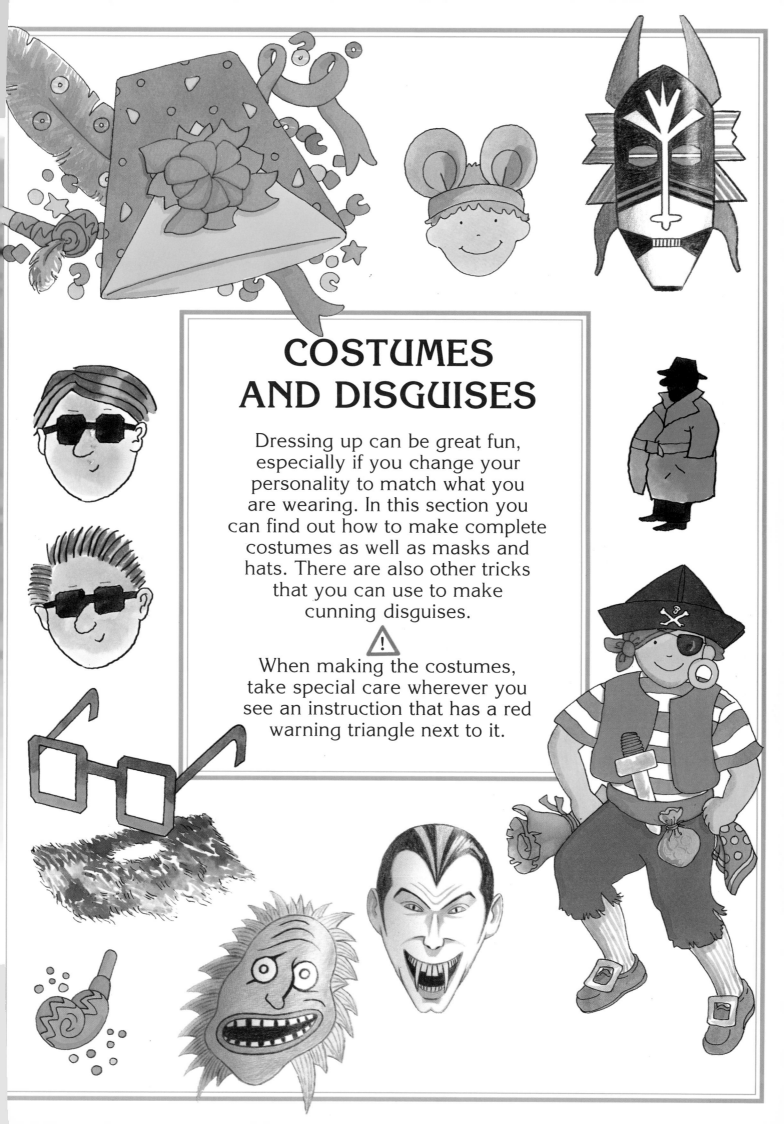

COSTUMES AND DISGUISES

Dressing up can be great fun, especially if you change your personality to match what you are wearing. In this section you can find out how to make complete costumes as well as masks and hats. There are also other tricks that you can use to make cunning disguises.

⚠

When making the costumes, take special care wherever you see an instruction that has a red warning triangle next to it.

Quick disguises

These techniques were developed by spies, to help them avoid capture by their enemies. You might like to try them for yourself, either on their own or using several disguises at the same time.

One-armed spy

You could wear a coat like the one on the right so that you look as though you have one arm. Before putting on the coat, tuck a sleeve inside a pocket. When you put it on, place your arm into the coat's free arm only. Button the coat, holding the concealed arm across your body.

Sleeve in pocket.

Arm inside coat.

Two way scarf

To make a quick-change scarf you will need two scarves that are the same size and shape, but which have different patterns. Pin them together and then carefully stitch all around the four sides, using a needle and thread. When you have finished stitching, remove the pins.

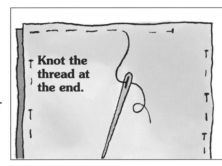

Knot the thread at the end.

Change your walk

A good trick that spies use is to pretend to have a stiff leg or a limp. To ensure that they don't forget that they have a stiff leg, or start to limp on the wrong foot, they do certain things, which are outlined below. You might like to follow these tips to ensure that your limp is always consistent.

• To make yourself limp, put a small stone in one shoe.

• For a stiff leg, put a ruler at the back of one knee and tie it on with a scarf or string. Then you will not be able to bend it. Wear long trousers or a very long skirt to hide the ruler.

Q. What food do secret agents like most?
A. Mince spies.

Change your shape

The towel makes your shoulders look higher.

With disguise

Without disguise

Hat and towel in bag.

To raise your shoulders, lay a small towel behind your neck, as shown above. Then put a coat on over it. This will help you look like an older person with muscular shoulders.

To change your appearance even more, you could also wear a hat or a scarf. Carry a folded plastic bag in your pocket. Later you can carry the hat and towel in the bag.

To make yourself look fatter, tie a small cushion around your middle, using a belt or some string. To conceal the cushion, button a coat over it, or wear a very big sweater.

Change your looks

You could try these tricks to alter your hairstyle or the shape of your face temporarily.

White hair

To lighten your hair and eyebrows, put talcum powder on them. If your hair is blonde it will look completely white.

Different hairstyle

Comb your hair a different way. Also, you could slick it back or part it in a different place.

Changed eyebrows

Rub bits of damp soap or white face paint into your eyebrows to cover them. Then draw new eyebrows with black crayon.

Face shade

To make your face paler, rub some talcum powder on it. Rub it in gently and don't use too much. Use cocoa powder to make your face look browner.

Missing tooth

For a missing tooth paint black tooth enamel (available from theatrical costume shops) on a tooth, or rub it with a black wax crayon.

Stubble

To create stubble, mix dabs of dark blue and black paint with some moisturizing cream. Then rub a little on your face gently, so that it looks as if you need a shave.

Lumpy face

To give your face a lumpy appearance, put segments of orange between your teeth and cheeks. To make lumpy jowls you should put the orange next to your lower teeth.

Wrinkle lines

Draw wrinkle lines with a dark pencil. Smile very hard and wrinkle your forehead to see where the lines should go. Then mark them in.

Mouse ears

Most of the instructions shown here tell you how to make a set of mouse ears. By adapting the basic idea, you can make the ears of other animals, such as pigs, dogs or sheep. When you wear the ears, you could use face paints to draw the animal's markings on your face.

Q. What do you do if a mouse stops breathing?

A. Give it mouse to mouse resuscitation.

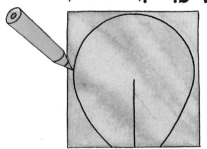

When you cut out the ears, the tracing paper should be on top.

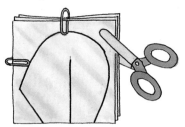

1. Lay some greaseproof paper onto the mouse ear template that is on page 94. Then trace the outline and the middle line with a pencil.

2. Line up the tracing with two paper squares and secure it with paper clips. Cut along all the drawn lines carefully, then remove the tracing.

3. Carefully trace the middles of the ears from the template onto some pink paper. Cut them out in the same way as the outer ears.

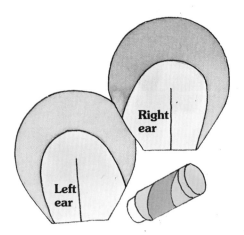

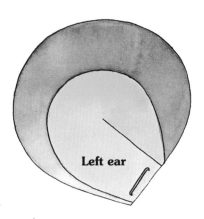

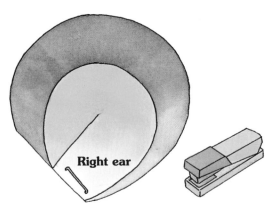

4. Turn one of the ear middles over. Glue both of them to the outer ears, matching the corners and the middle lines.

5. Lift the left side of the left ear and overlap it onto the right side, so that it looks like the one shown here. Then staple them together.

6. Lift the right side of the right ear and overlap it onto the left side. Staple together both parts of the ear at their bases.

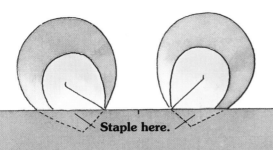

Staple here.

Fold the bottom up to the top.

7. Mark the middle of the paper strip. Staple the left and right ears at each side about 8cm (3½in) apart.

8. Fold the band over itself to hide the staples. Fit the band around the head and secure it with paper clips.

To prevent staples from catching on your hair cover them with adhesive tape.

Using face paints, draw a round nose and some whiskers on your face.

Cat ears

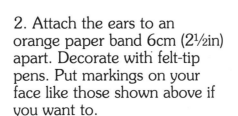

1. Cut out two cat ears from orange paper using the cat ears template on page 94. Turn in, but do not fold, the inner corners by 3cm (1½in). Staple them at the base.

2. Attach the ears to an orange paper band 6cm (2½in) apart. Decorate with felt-tip pens. Put markings on your face like those shown above if you want to.

Other ideas to try

Pig ears

Using pink paper, make two ears in the same way that you would make cat ears.

Draw on a snout, or use a section from an egg carton painted with nose holes. Attach the snout to your face using elastic.

Dog ears

Cut two long floppy ears, using stiff black paper. Allow them to hang down. Draw on a black eye, nose and whiskers.

Sheep ears

Cut two floppy black ears. Attach them to a white headband which has balls of white cotton attached to it.

Draw on a black nose.

Party hats

To make party hats you need large squares of paper. Patterned wrapping paper is ideal. You could use newspaper instead and decorate the hats on one side, using paints or felt-tip pens.

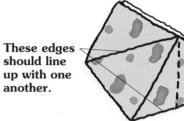

You will need

• Felt-tip pens or paints
• Paper 40 x 40cm (16 x 16in)
• Scraps of eye-catching paper, such as silver paper or crêpe paper

Pill box hat

These edges should line up with one another.

1. Take the square of paper and lay it flat. Ideally, it should have a pattern on one side only.

2. With the plain side facing up, fold two of the corners together.

3. Fold a sharp corner across to the opposite edge so that the top and bottom edges line up.

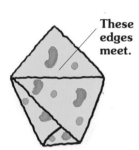

These edges meet.

This is the other side.

4. Fold the other sharp corner across in the same way as you did before. Then turn the paper around.

5. Fold the top corner up over the edges. Turn the paper over and do the same again.

You could cut scrap paper into the shape of feathers and attach it to the hat.

Other ideas

Bird mask

Leave the last corner, on the side with no folds, pointing down to make the beak. Paint it yellow. Cut out nostrils so that you can see through the holes.

Tape some feather-shaped paper to the top for plumage.

Include huge eyes on your mask.

Clown hat

To complete the effect of a clown hat, make a crêpe paper fringe for the hair.

Stick a paper flower on the front.

To make the fringe

Use a strip of crêpe paper about 15 x 30cm (6 x 12in). Make lots of cuts along one edge. Glue the other edge inside the rim of your hat. Remember to leave a space for your face.

Crown

You will need
• Four square pieces of paper
20 x 20cm (8 x 8in)

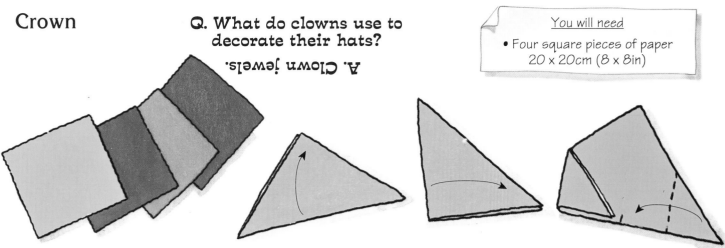

1. Take four identical squares of paper. Turn the first square so that a corner is facing you.

2. With the underside facing up, fold the bottom corner to the top corner.

3. Fold the triangular shape in half. Then fold in the side corners to meet the middle.

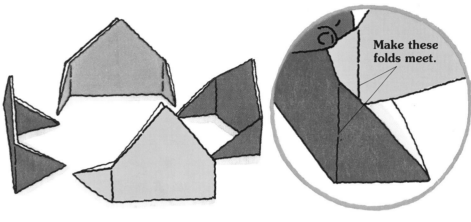

Make these folds meet.

4. Fold all your squares in the same way. Then stand them in a square with the corners pointing in, ready to join together.

5. To link the separate pieces of paper together slot each corner inside the one next to it, making sure that the folds meet.

Other ideas

Crown of jewels

Glue on gum drops or bright buttons as jewels. Alternatively, crumple up tiny pieces of cooking foil and attach them to the crown.

Rich gold crown

Use paper that is decorated on both sides. Glue gold doilies to one side. Trim off any overlapping bits. Fold each square with the doily side down.

Bend the inner points into the middle and tape them together.

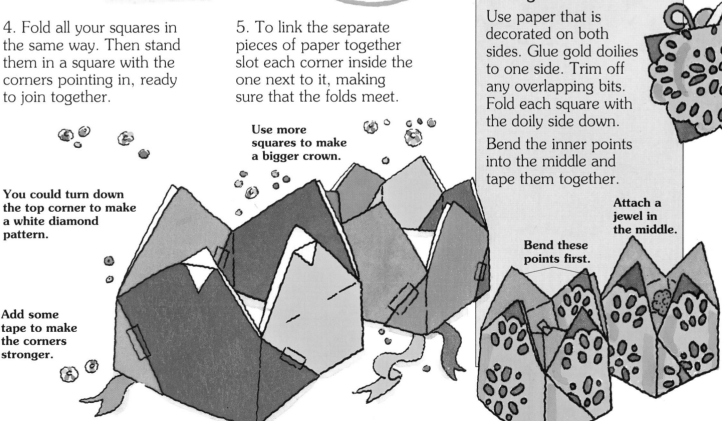

Use more squares to make a bigger crown.

You could turn down the top corner to make a white diamond pattern.

Add some tape to make the corners stronger.

Bend these points first.

Attach a jewel in the middle.

Pirate

Bigbeard's missing bullion
Lies on the Isle of Gore
If you find his hidden gold
You'll be rich for evermore.

To make this outfit you will need to cut up some of your old clothes. Before you start, check with grown-ups that they are happy for you to do this. Instead, you could buy cheap old clothes from a charity shop or a rummage sale. You might like to buy some cheap old brooches and earrings, to wear with your costume. You can pretend that you've stolen them from other voyagers.

Q. Where do pirates go when they have some free time?

A. Leisure island.

Pirate's hat

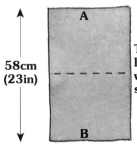

58cm (23in)

This crease line shows where the fold should go.

1. Fold the piece of paper in half, as shown above, so that edge A meets edge B exactly.

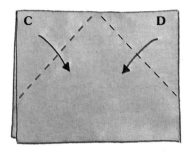

2. Now fold the points marked C and D so that they meet in the middle.

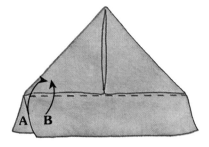

3. Fold up the edges B and A on either side to complete the shape of the hat.

The skull and bones should be the same size as those shown here.

4. To make a skull and crossbones fold some white paper in half. Draw half a skull and a bone on it.

5. Cut out the skull and the crossbones, using scissors. Draw in the features on the face, using a black felt-tip pen.

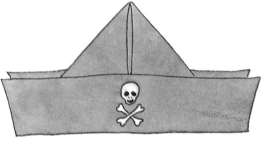

6. Glue the skull and crossbones shapes onto the middle of the turn up on the front of your hat.

Dagger

1. Cut out a rounded blade and handle from thin cardboard. Cover both pieces with cooking foil using tape.

2. Stick on the handle, as shown, with double-sided tape. Wind some string around the handle and tape the ends.

Shoe buckles

1. Begin by cutting two 5cm (2in) squares from a piece of thin cardboard.

2. Using a ruler, measure 1cm (½in) from the outer bottom edges. Cut to the top corners, as shown.

3. Measure and mark 1cm (½in) for the outer edges of the buckles.

4. Pierce the cardboard with the sharpened end of a pencil. Insert the blade of the scissors and cut out the middles.

5. Cover your buckles with cooking foil. Tie on fine elastic loops, large enough to slip on over shoes.

Q. What toys do pirates like playing with most?

A. Yo-ho-yos.

Costume tips
- Add a moustache or a scar using face paints.
- To make the hat larger or smaller adjust the size of the black paper.
- Make a small hole in the eye patch so that you can see out of it.

Cut an eye patch from black paper. Attach fine elastic to fit around your head.

Knot a headscarf around your head.

Tie a loop of thread on a curtain ring and hang it from your ear.

Cut up an old T-shirt to make a sleeveless jacket.

Use a long scarf as a cummerbund.

You could carry some coins in a handkerchief, attached to your waistband.

Cut off, or roll up, a pair of jeans at the knee.

White knee socks are ideal for this costume.

57

Printing on cloth

You can brighten up old clothes by printing vivid designs onto them. For the best results, use fabric paints, which you can buy from art shops. They are fairly expensive, so buy just two or three different shades, and mix some of each together, to create various effects. To help you to get good results when you are printing see the "Printing tips" section on the opposite page, before you start work.

You will need
- Fabric paints
- Waterproof inks
- Pieces of cloth • Old clothes
- Clay for clay blocks
- Rags and string for rag prints
- Candle for wax and dye patterns • Expanded polystyrene, cardboard and pins for cardboard blocks
- Long wooden stick or bamboo, some string, a needle and thread for wall hangings
- Pencil • Paintbrush
- Plenty of newspaper

Clay blocks

1. Shape some clay into a square block. Make lots of patterns or shapes in one side by pressing the end of a pencil into the clay.

2. Pour paint onto a tray or plate. Press the block, pattern side down, onto the paint. Then print your pattern onto the cloth you want to decorate.

Rag prints

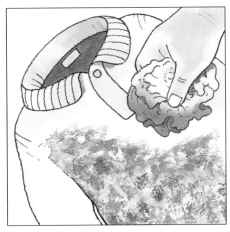

Use some old rags and lengths of string, dipped in different paints and pressed on a garment, to create some abstract patterns.

Cardboard blocks

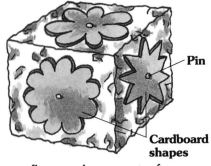

Pin

Cardboard shapes

Cut a flower shape out of thick cardboard. Push a pin through the middle and then into a block of thick expanded polystyrene.

Printing on shoes

To decorate white canvas shoes, first stuff them with newspaper. Brush fabric paint over the cardboard block and print the shape on the shoes.

T-shirts

You might like to print your name on a T-shirt.

Put folded newspaper inside a T-shirt to stop the dye from going through to the other side. Use a stencil and some fabric paint to print a pattern.

Wax and dye

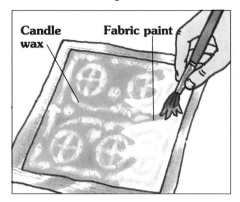

Draw a pattern on a piece of cloth with a white candle, pressing down very hard. Brush ink or dye over the cloth. It will remain white where the candle lines are.

Patched jeans

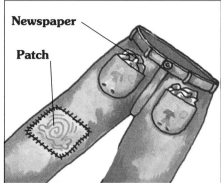

To create decorated patched jeans, print fabric paint on their pockets or print on fabric patches and sew them on. Put newspaper beneath the jeans before you start.

Printing tips

- Before you start printing, protect your work area and other belongings by putting lots of newspaper beneath the garment that you are going to decorate.

- Make sure that the clothes that you will print on are clean and dry.

- To check that your printing block gives good results, print on a scrap piece of cloth before you use it to decorate a piece of clothing. This way, you will avoid spoiling any clothes.

- For the best results, print onto cotton cloth.

Handkerchiefs

You could print names or initials made from stencils on handkerchiefs to make presents. Alternatively, you could sew the initials into the handkerchief, using a needle and thread.

Q. What did the boot seller say to the fly?

A. Shoe!

A complete wardrobe

The display below shows some of the impressive effects that you can create using the decorative methods shown on these pages.

Wall hangings

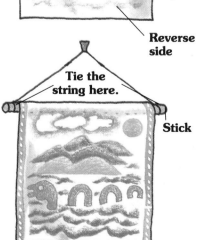

1. Using fabric paint, print onto a large white cloth. A piece of old shirt is good for this. Fold over about 3cm (1in) at the top and stitch the edge down, as shown above.

2. Push a long stick or piece of bamboo through the stitched pocket. Tie the ends of a piece of string to the stick or bamboo and hang the picture up.

Masks

In some parts of the world people wear masks for superstitious reasons or during religious ceremonies or festivals, such as carnivals. The actors in some traditional types of drama wear them too, to help show the identities of the characters.

Q. What type of insect devours masks?

A. A mask-eat-o.

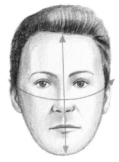

1. Start by measuring the face of the person who will wear the mask. Measure from the hairline to the chin, and around the face from ear to ear.

2. Draw the face shape onto your cardboard, according to your measurements. The mask will look very wide, because of the curve of the face.

3. Plot the features of the mask in pencil. Then decorate it according to your preferred design. Finally, cut it out carefully, using scissors.

4. Mark the positions for two holes, about 1cm (½in) in from the widest points on either side of the mask (at about ear height).

5. Use the point of a pencil to make small holes in the mask. Push elastic into the holes and tie it in place with knots.

6. Work out where eye holes should go so that you will be able to see. Carefully mark the positions for the eye holes with a pencil.

7. Pierce tiny eye holes in the mask. The holes do not have to be in the same place as the eyes of the mask design.

Mask styles

Exaggerated outlines can be drawn around the basic shape to make masks like those on the right. Two of these designs are based on traditional masks. The other is made up, to look like Count Dracula.

Vampire mask

Traditional mask used for Japanese plays.

This one is based on a mask made by North American Indians.

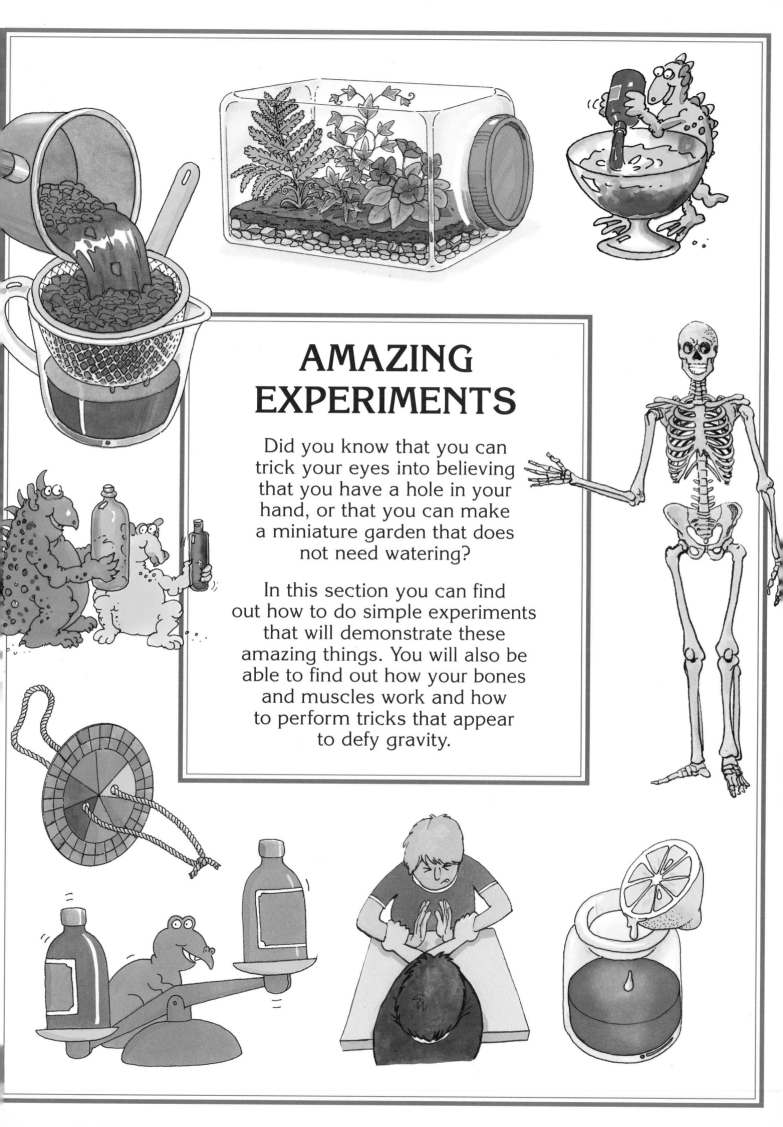

AMAZING EXPERIMENTS

Did you know that you can trick your eyes into believing that you have a hole in your hand, or that you can make a miniature garden that does not need watering?

In this section you can find out how to do simple experiments that will demonstrate these amazing things. You will also be able to find out how your bones and muscles work and how to perform tricks that appear to defy gravity.

Tests with water

Water's surface has a type of skin. This is because the particles, called molecules, that make up the water pull each other together. By carrying out a few experiments you can see how this works.

Fill a glass with water. Put a needle on a small piece of tissue paper and lay it gently on the water. Eventually the tissue will sink, but the needle will stay where it is.

If you look closely at the surface of the water you will see that it is dented all around the needle. The water looks as if it has a skin and the needle is resting on it.

At first, the tissue paper sits on top of the water with the needle on it.

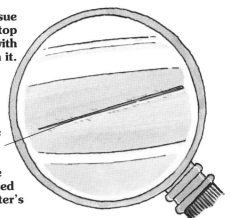

The tissue paper has sunk, but the needle is supported by the water's surface.

Surface tension

The needle experiment shows that the surface of water is strong enough to support some things. This strength is called "surface tension".

You can sometimes see insects called pond skaters skimming on a pond's surface. They can walk on water because its surface tension is strong enough to support them.

Bulging water

Fill a cup to the very top with water, then gently add a little more, so that the water rises, but does not spill over the edge of the cup.

The water looks as if it will overflow, but it doesn't. Its surface tension is strong enough to hold it in place and stop it from overflowing.

Water's skin is strong enough to allow drops of it to cling to things, such as a tap, before they get so heavy that they fall.

Watch how water drips from a tap and look at the shape of the water drops. The water's skin holds drops together and gives them their shape.

Water magic

1. Suck some water into a straw and put your finger on the mouth end to hold the water in the straw. Take your finger off to let some drops fall onto a clean plastic surface.

2. Look at the shape of the drops of water. Now dip one end of a match into some dishwashing liquid and touch each drop of water. The panel on the right explains what happens to them.

What happens?

The surface tension of the water makes the drops of water stand up. When you add dishwashing liquid to the water, it makes the surface of the water more elastic, so the drops spread out more.

Blowing bubbles

When you blow bubbles, water really does look as if it has a skin and you can see how elastic it can be.

1. Make a mixture by stirring dishwashing liquid into a cup of water. The liquid makes the water's skin more elastic, so that you can blow better bubbles.

2. Make a loop out of a piece of thin wire and dip it into the bubble mixture. You will see a thin film of liquid stretched across the loop. Now start blowing bubbles.

3. Blow gently, then harder, and the film of liquid will stretch. You might be able to blow huge bubbles, depending on how much dishwashing liquid you use.

Q. What animal can write underwater?
A. A ball-point pen-guin.

By blowing long and very hard, you will be able to blow a long stream of small bubbles.

Bubbles always float down, because their skin makes them heavier than air.

Bubbles with weak skins pop, like the one that hit this man's glasses.

Amazing liquids

It's surprising what interesting things you can do with liquids. For instance, the cocktail on the right is made of three ingredients which settle in layers. You could make these liquid tricks for yourself. A word of warning though: don't drink the liquids after you've done your experiments – they'll taste horrible.

You will need

- Carbonated drink • Fruit cordial
- 3 tablespoons of cream
- Variety of liquids, as shown in the section below called "Density test"
- Water • Salt • Food dye

Cocktail recipe

DON'T STIR IT!

1. Put a small amount of carbonated drink, such as cola, in a glass.

2. Pour in enough of the fruit cordial to cover the bottom of the glass.

3. Add the dyed cream gently, one spoon at a time. The liquids will sit in layers.

Why is the drink layered?

The liquids are in layers because the ingredients have different weights, or densities. The syrup sinks to the bottom because it is denser, or heavier than the carbonated drink. Cream is lighter, or less dense, so it stays on top.

Density test

Can you find out which of these liquids are denser than water and which are less dense? Drop a spoonful of each one into a jar of water and see if it sinks or floats. Check your results on page 96.

IF YOU WEIGH TWO IDENTICAL CONTAINERS FILLED WITH DIFFERENT THINGS, THE DENSER THING WILL WEIGH MORE.

Q. What can fly under water?

A. A parrot in a submarine.

Bottle fountain

1. These three monsters are making a magic bottle fountain. Find two bottles that are identical, some water, food dye and salt. Wide-necked plastic bottles are the best to use.

2. Fill the first bottle with cold tap water mixed with food dye. Make sure that you use enough food dye to make the water look very bright. That way, you will be able to see the experiment clearly.

> THE DYED WATER RISES BECAUSE IT IS LESS DENSE THAN THE SALT WATER.

3. Fill the second bottle with water mixed with three tablespoons of salt. So that the salt mixes in easily, use warm water, but let it cool before you conduct your experiment.

4. Hold a piece of cardboard over the top of the salt water bottle. Holding the cardboard tightly, turn the bottle upside down. Balance the salt water bottle on top of the other one.

5. Hold both bottles carefully and get somebody to remove the cardboard slowly and gently. Make sure that you keep the mouths of the bottles together, or you'll spill the water.

> YOU MAY BE ABLE TO SEE SOME WATER MOVING DOWN. THIS IS THE DENSE SALT WATER SINKING TO THE BOTTOM.

Did you know?

Things float more easily in dense (heavy) liquids. This is why it is easier to swim in the sea. The salty water is denser than ordinary water so it helps to keep you afloat. Also, because of the salt in sea water, ships float more easily when they are on the ocean than when they are in a river. In the sea they sit higher out of the water than when they are in fresh water.

Q. What do you get if you cross the ocean with a paper boat?

A. Wet.

> THE DEAD SEA IN THE MIDDLE EAST CONTAINS A LOT OF SALT, SO IT IS VERY EASY TO FLOAT IN IT.

Skeletons

Animals, such as dogs, birds and humans, have skeletons inside the body. Others, such as crabs and insects, have skeletons on the outside. However, some animals don't have any skeletons. On these pages you can find out how all these different systems work.

Why animals have skeletons

IF ANIMALS DID NOT HAVE SKELETONS, THEY WOULD NOT BE ABLE TO STAND ON LEGS. THEY WOULD COLLAPSE UNDER THEIR OWN WEIGHT.

1. To see what an animal's body would do without a skeleton, make a giraffe out of model dough. See if it can stand up.

2. The giraffe collapses because it doesn't have a frame to stop the soft model dough from bending.

3. If you put plastic drinking straws in its legs and neck, they will act like a skeleton, supporting the model dough.

How do you move?

The skeleton inside your body is made up of over 200 bones which are joined together by tough bands, called ligaments. The places where bones meet are called joints.

Your shoulders and hips have ball-shaped joints fitted into rounded sockets. These enable you to move your arms and legs in most directions.

The two bones in your lower arm join your wrist to make a pivot joint, so that you can turn your hands over.

Your elbow joint works like a door hinge and can only move up and down.

Your skull is made of curved bones that are fixed together. They make a helmet of bone to protect your brain.

The ribs in your chest form a cage which protects your heart and your lungs.

Without joints you would not be able to bend or move. This is because your arms and legs are moved by muscles pulling on bones on either side of the joints.

Working muscles

Hold one of your arms out straight and put your other hand just above the elbow.

Lift up the lower part of your arm. You will feel a muscle above your elbow, called the biceps, bulging out as it pulls together (contracts).

The biceps becomes shorter as it draws up the lower part of your arm.

When you lower your arm, muscles at the back contract. The biceps gets longer and thinner.

Muscle strength

Muscles that you use a lot are often stronger than the ones you rarely use. To prove this, ask a friend to press both hands together tightly, as in first picture on the right. Try to pull them apart by gripping each wrist and pulling out.

It is difficult to pull the hands apart because the muscles you are using are not very strong.

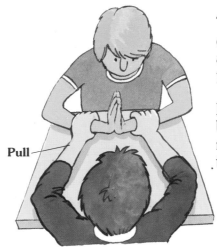

Pull

Try the test again by crossing your hands over and pushing your partner's hands apart.

It is easier to do because you use the muscles often, so they are strong.

Push

Outside skeletons

Crab　　Prawn

Insects, spiders, centipedes, millipedes and shellfish, such as crabs, all have their skeletons on the outside of their bodies.

The muscles are inside the skeleton. Legs are attached to the skeleton.

By looking closely at an insect, such as the ones shown above, you can see that the outside of its body is hard. This hard surface is the insect's skeleton.

An outside skeleton gives these animals good protection against enemies.

If you touch a woodlouse it curls up and its whole body becomes a hard ball. Its outside skeleton fits together to provide it with very good protection.

Animals without skeletons

Muscles cannot work unless they have something to push and pull against. Worms have no skeleton, so their muscles work in a different way.

Their muscles are built around the edge of their bodies, while in the middle they are made of fluid. To move, their muscles push against the fluid. The picture on the right shows you the two types of muscle that worms have to move them along. The pictures below show you how the muscles work to make them move.

Q. What seafood do weight-lifters like most?

A. Mussels.

Circular muscles are made in a circle around the body. These contract and push against the fluid to make the body become long and thin.

Fluid

Long muscles run the length of the body. These push against the fluid to make the body become short and fat.

1. Long muscles make the back of the body bulge out. This causes bristles to grip the earth at the back.

2. Circular muscles contract at the back. The body becomes long and thin and the bristles stop gripping.

3. Long muscles work at the front. Front bristles grip.

4. Long muscles along the body contract. The body becomes short and pulls the back forward.

Science magic

You will need lots of breath to produce the surprising results shown in the tests on this page. Their results are so unexpected that it will seem as if you are performing magic tricks.

You will need
(for magic tube and anti-gravity funnel)
• Table tennis ball • Pencil
• Paper 20 x 10cm (8 x 4in)
• Circle of thin cardboard 10cm (4in) across
• Drinking straw • Glue
• Adhesive tape • Scissors

Magic tube

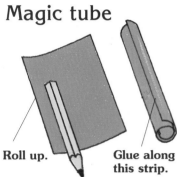

Roll up. **Glue along this strip.**

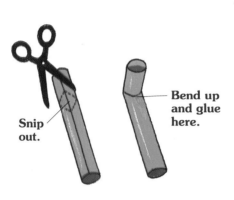

Snip out. **Bend up and glue here.**

1. Put a pencil down on the edge of the paper. Roll up the paper around it. Stick the edge with glue to make a long tube and then shake out the pencil.

2. Make a snip in the tube, near one end. Make another snip to cut out a V-shape. Bend the end, and put glue on the join. Let the glue dry.

3. To perform the trick, hold the table tennis ball above the end of the straw. Blow hard and let go of the ball. It will stay where you put it.

Anti-gravity funnel

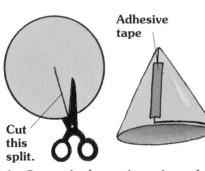

Adhesive tape

Cut this split.

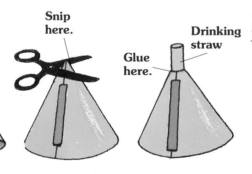

Snip here. **Glue here.** **Drinking straw**

1. Cut a slit from the edge of the cardboard circle to the middle. Curl the circle up to make a cone. Stick the edges together with adhesive tape.

2. Snip off the cone's top. Push a 4cm (2in) piece of drinking straw though the hole so that its tip goes inside the cone. Glue it to the cone and leave it to dry.

3. Point the funnel up and put the table tennis ball into it. As you blow, point the funnel down. The ball defies gravity and stays in the funnel.

How the tricks work

Fast moving air has less push, or pressure, than slow moving air. When you blow, the air coming through the straw moves faster than the air on the other side of the table tennis ball.

The slower moving air pushes the ball to the straw, and this keeps it fixed in its original place.

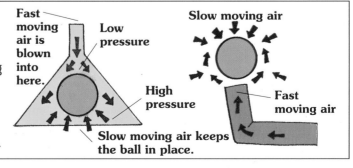

Fast moving air is blown into here. **Low pressure** **High pressure** **Slow moving air keeps the ball in place.**

Slow moving air **Fast moving air**

Magic disk

Can you believe that this disk can be made to turn white for a few seconds? Follow the instructions shown below and you'll find out how to do it.

You will need
- Cup with a wide top
- Paints or felt-tip pens or pencil crayons
- Pencil • String • Thick cardboard

Draw here.

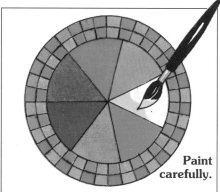

Paint carefully.

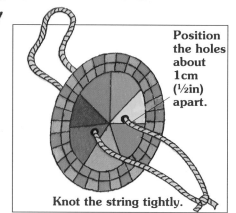

Position the holes about 1cm (½in) apart.

Knot the string tightly.

1. Place your cup on some thick cardboard and draw around it. Cut around the line with scissors to make a circle.

2. Using a pencil, divide your disk into the shapes shown above. Then paint the sections exactly as shown.

3. Make two holes in the circle. Push a piece of string, about 1m (3ft) long, through the holes and knot the ends together.

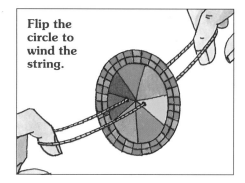

Flip the circle to wind the string.

4. Hold the loops of string as shown here. Flip the circle around and around to twist up the string. Pull your hands apart to make the string unravel and the disk spin.

Why it works

When the disk spins you see the patterns but they get mixed up in your brain. The disk looks a sort of dull white.

Q. What do disks do when they get together?

A. They have a disk-ussion.

WHEN YOU LOOK AT A RAINBOW, IT IS MADE UP MOSTLY OF THESE SHADES.

Instead of putting string through the disk, you might prefer to push a pencil through its middle and use it as a spinning top.

Sour things

When you taste foods and drinks you can tell whether they are sweet or sour. Things such as lemons and vinegar taste sour because they contain acids. You can do a simple test to see if a food or drink contains acid, using the water from a boiled red cabbage.

Q. What food do porcupines like most?
A. Prickled onions.

Tasting sourness

By tasting different sorts of food and drink, you can tell which might be acidic. Below are some of the things that you could try. Before you taste them, see if you can guess which ones will taste sour. You will probably find that some of them taste as you expected, but others do not.

Before you taste each different liquid, rinse your mouth with fresh water. That way, their tastes will not affect each other, and your results will not be spoiled.

Vinegar

Carbonated drink

Milk

Water

Orange

Salt

Yogurt

Sugar

Grapefruit

You could make a chart to record your findings.

Red cabbage test

You will need
• Half a red cabbage
• Assortment of things to taste and test • Water
• Saucepan • Strainer
• Heatproof water container
• Jars or glasses

1. You can make red cabbage water to help you test for acid in food. Tear the red cabbage leaves into little pieces and put them in a saucepan of water.

Cook the cabbage in the water for ten to fifteen minutes. Then take it off the heat and leave it to cool.

2. When the water has cooled pour the cabbage through a strainer, catching the water in a container beneath.

You will not need the cabbage again after you have strained its water.

3. Look at the cabbage water to see what shade of purple it is. Pour a little of the water into each of your jars.

4. Add some lemon juice to one of the jars of cabbage water. You will see that the appearance of the water will change.

5. One by one, put each of the other things that taste sour into jars of cabbage water. Do they all turn the water pink?

6. Put the things that don't taste sour into separate jars of cabbage water. Do they turn the water pink?

Test results

The cabbage water changes from purple to pink when you add acidic things to it. Things that are not acidic will either leave the cabbage water purple or turn it green. The shades that occur will vary. You might like to record your findings on a chart.

You will find that some of the things that are acidic, such as carbonated drinks, do not taste sour because there is lots of sugar in them.

Q. What do you get if you mix grapes, water and a bomb?
A. Wine-amite.

Hungry acids

Acids will eat away at things that they come into contact with. In fact, strong acids are dangerous to living things because they will eat away at their bodies.

To see an acid at work, leave an old coin in some cola overnight. You will find that the acid in the cola is strong enough to strip the dirt from the coin.

Warning: do not drink the cola after you have used it to clean the coin. ⚠️

Pickled food

Keeping food in vinegar is called pickling. The acid in vinegar stops food from going bad, so you can keep it for a long time. Pickling changes the taste of food. It is most commonly used to preserve vegetables and to make chutneys and pickles. Even if it is used on sweet things, such as fruits, it makes them taste sour.

Q. Where do chutneys go when they are ill?
A. To hos-pickle.

Q. How do you describe a man who is standing in a mixture of tomatoes, vinegar and onions?
A. You say that he is in a pickle.

Eye tricks

Sometimes your eyes play tricks on you so that you think you are seeing something that is not there at all. To prove this, you could try the tricks shown here, called optical illusions. You will be surprised by the results. After you have tried them, you might like to draw them for yourself and test them out on your friends.

You will need
• Ruler
• Small pieces of thin cardboard or paper
• Paper 30 x 20cm (12 x 8in)
• Pencil
• Felt-tip pens

Bending lines

Look at the patterns of lines on the right. In the top pattern, do the long green lines bend out near their ends? In the lower pattern, do the green lines get wider in the middle?

To check whether the green lines are bent, put the edge of a ruler against each one.

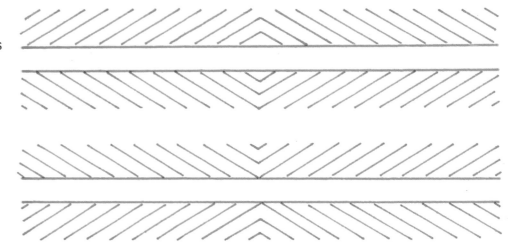

Tricky top hat

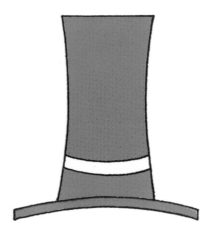

When you look at this top hat, is the brim wider than the height? Or is the height bigger than the brim? Measure the height and the width of the brim to find whether the appearance is misleading.

Deceptive shapes

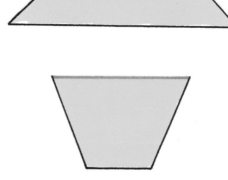

In this illusion, is the red line on the shape at the top longer, or shorter, than the red line on the lower shape? The different overall shapes trick your brain into believing that the red lines are of different lengths.

Ladder lengths

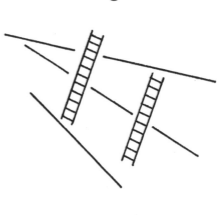

Are these ladders the same length, or is one longer than the other? The lines make the one on the right look as if it is closer to you, but the ladder on the left looks longer because it breaks out of the upper lines.

Arrowhead teaser

Which of the red lines is longer? In the shape nearer to the top of the page, the black arrowheads point in to make the overall shape fairly long. In the second picture the arrowheads enclose the line and make the overall shape compact. You will probably need to measure the two red lines to be sure which one is longer.

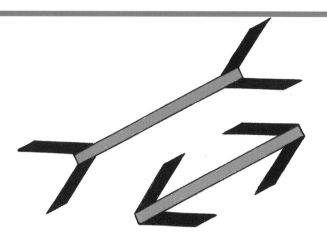

Quick tricks

Here are some quick tricks that you can play on your eyes. Test them on yourself first, then get your friends to do them.

Seeing double

Hold one finger of each hand up in front of your eyes, about 20cm (8in) from your face. Stare hard at something beyond your fingers, not at them. You will see ghostly fingers in front of your eyes.

Look at your fingers and the ghostly fingers will disappear.

Floating sausage finger

Hold one finger of each hand up horizontally, 10cm (4in) in front of your eyes. If you stare hard at the gap between your fingers, you will see a short sausage-like finger appear between them. The sausage has a nail on both ends.

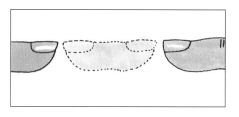

The floating sausage will look a little like the one in this picture.

Hole in the hand

Make a tube by rolling up a piece of paper, 30 x 20cm (12 x 8in). Keeping both eyes open, hold the tube up to your right eye and look down it. Hold your left hand up beside the tube, about 10cm (4in) from the end, and stare hard down the tube. You should see a hole in your hand.

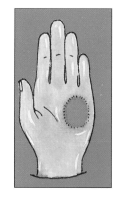

You should be able to see a hole in anything you use for this trick.

Why the quick tricks work

For the first two tricks you concentrate on things that are close up while your eyes look into the distance. Each eye sees a different picture, which your brain tries to fit together. The result is that you see something that doesn't exist.

In the third trick, your eyes are forced to work on their own, instead of as a pair, so you see two different things. However, because your brain is used to them working together, it tries to fit the two different images together.

Bottle garden

Like all living things, plants need water in order to survive. Plants get their water by absorbing it, either when it rains or when they are watered. However, you can make a garden that never needs watering, simply by following the instructions shown here. The things you will need are all available from gardening shops.

You will need
- Damp soil
- Charcoal
- Pebbles
- Large glass bottle or jar with a lid
- Small plants, such as ivy, fern and African violet
- Large spoon or planting trowel

Making the bottle garden

To make your bottle garden, lay the glass bottle or jar on its side. Fill it with layers of pebbles, charcoal and damp soil in the order shown in the picture on the right.

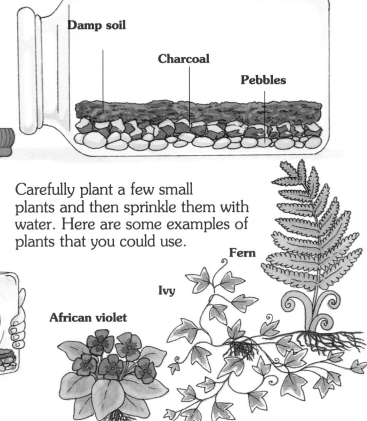

Carefully plant a few small plants and then sprinkle them with water. Here are some examples of plants that you could use.

Fern

Ivy

African violet

You could make a planting trowel by tying a spoon to a stick, as shown in this picture.

Q. What type of entertainment do flowers like most?

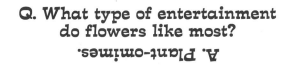

A. Plant-omimes.

Put the lid on the bottle tightly and leave it in a warm, light place. The plants should keep on growing healthily.

The plants absorb water from the soil through their roots. The water is drawn up the plant until it reaches the leaves. Drops of water form on the leaves, then drop onto the soil. Then the roots absorb the water again.

Roots

TOYS AND GAMES

You can have fun making the toys and games in this section from ordinary things that you probably have around your home, such as old plastic bottles, shoe boxes, candles and potatoes. Even if you need to buy new materials, they will not be expensive.

Every now and then you will have to cut something out or heat it in an oven. To warn you to take extra care, a red triangle is shown wherever this happens. You might like to ask an adult to help you with these stages.

Delta wing

These paper planes are fairly simple to make and fly. To ensure that you get the best results, follow these instructions closely and use good quality writing paper or photocopy paper.

Q. Why did the jumbo jet go to the doctor?

A. It had an air-pain.

Making your delta wing

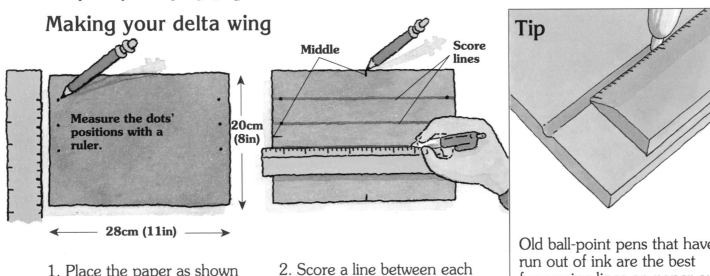

Measure the dots' positions with a ruler.

28cm (11in)

20cm (8in)

Middle

Score lines

Tip

Old ball-point pens that have run out of ink are the best for scoring lines on paper or cardboard. They run smoothly and do not cause marks, scratches or rips.

1. Place the paper as shown here. Make pencil dots 4cm, 8cm and 12cm (1½in, 3in and 4½in) below the top edge, on both sides.

2. Score a line between each pair of dots, using a ball-point pen and a ruler. Then mark the middle of each edge of the paper with a pencil.

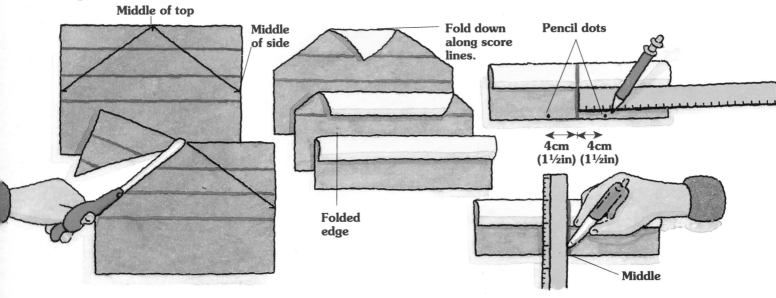

Middle of top

Middle of side

Fold down along score lines.

Pencil dots

Folded edge

4cm (1½in)   4cm (1½in)

Middle

3. Draw a line from the middle of each side to the middle of the top. Then cut along it.

4. Fold down the top edge along all the score lines you made earlier.

5. Mark the middle of the folded edge. Then score a line right down the middle.

6. Make two pencil dots on the bottom edge, 4cm (1½in) from the middle of the paper.

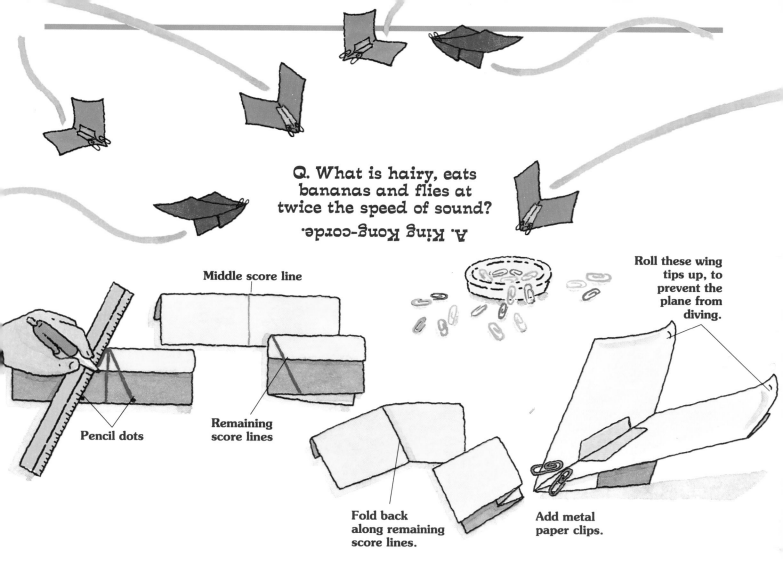

Q. What is hairy, eats bananas and flies at twice the speed of sound?

A. King Kong-corde.

Middle score line

Pencil dots

Remaining score lines

Fold back along remaining score lines.

Add metal paper clips.

Roll these wing tips up, to prevent the plane from diving.

7. Score a line up from each of the dots you made in stage 6 to the middle of the folded edge. Use a ruler to help you get the lines exactly right.

8. Turn the paper over. Fold it down the middle line. Then fold the wings back along the remaining score lines, to make the plane's triangular body.

9. Fold the wings back to make them stick out. Tape down the middle and add paper clips to the nose, to give the plane some weight.

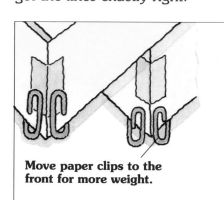

Move paper clips to the front for more weight.

Changing the balance

If the delta wing stalls, change its balance by moving the paper clips to the front. This will make the plane heavier at the front. If it dives, move the paper clips back so that it is less front-heavy.

Stall

Dive

Open-air flights

On a calm, dry day, you could try throwing your delta wing from an upstairs window, for a really long glide. To launch the delta wing, throw it quite fast. You could test fly it and adjust the balance as suggested above, before you try an open-air flight.

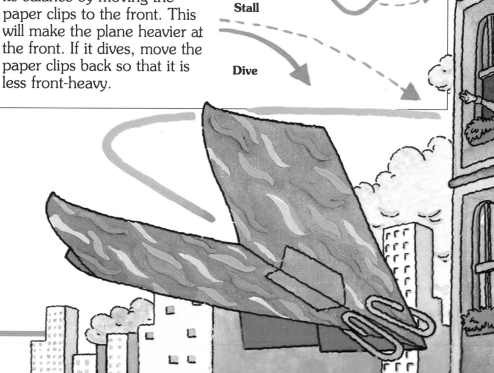

Origami

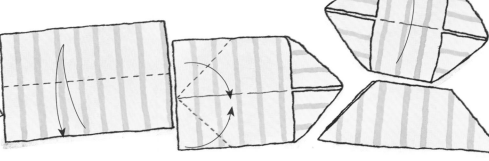

"Origami" is an ancient Japanese word that means "paper folding". You can use the techniques to make simple models, such as the ones shown on this page. If you enjoy doing origami, there is a more challenging project for you to do on pages 84-85. There are also instructions for how to make a paperfold kite on page 86.

You will need
• Large rectangle of thin paper, such as a sheet of newspaper or thin wrapping paper
• Felt-tip pens

Big bang

 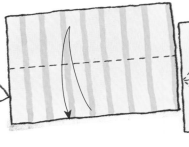

1. Take a sheet of paper. Thin paper such as newspaper is best as it is more likely to make a good loud bang.

2. Fold the long sides of the paper together and make a strong crease. Then unfold the paper.

3. Fold down each corner, matching one edge of the folded piece with the middle crease.

4. Make a fold along the middle crease, to make the shape shown above.

Banger duels

You could challenge your friends to duels, to see who can make the first bang after a count of three.

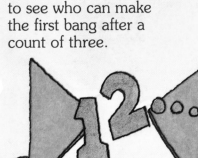

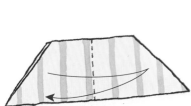 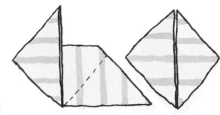

5. Fold the paper in half again from side to side, to make a strong crease. Then unfold it.

6. Fold the bottom corners so that the bottom edge meets the middle crease. Turn the paper over.

When you use your banger, have this edge facing you.

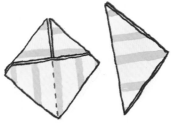  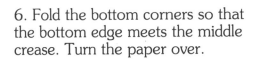

Alternatively, stand back to back with a friend, walk five paces away from each other, then see who can turn and draw first.

7. Fold the shape in half from side to side, as shown here. Then pick up the banger and hold it firmly at the open end.

8. Make sure the long edge is facing you. Then raise your hand and bring it down sharply. The paper will open with a bang.

78

Customized bangers

To create a range of bangers that give a variety of noises, make them in a selection of different sizes. You could also decorate them with words and designs, to make them more eye-catching.

Q. What hobby does Dracula like most?

A. Horror-gami.

Q. What do frogs read to find out about recent events?

A. Newts-papers.

Make your bangers as bright as you can.

Glue on silver lightning flashes.

Add glitter and sequins.

Write on noisy words.

You could draw clouds on your bangers.

ZAP!

CRACK!

WOOZ

Snowstorms

Tear up lots of small pieces of paper and tuck them inside the fold. When the banger snaps open the "snow" will scatter all over your victim.

Add stars.

BANG!

Be prepared to clear up afterwards.

Junk games

With help from the instructions on these pages you can turn old bits of junk, such as plastic drinks bottles or shoe boxes, into indoor games. Before you get to work on the junk, check that it isn't being saved for some other purpose.

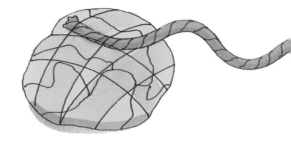

Catch cup

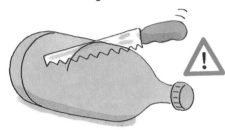

1. Using a bread knife, cut a large plastic bottle, about 15cm (6in) from its top.

2. Crush a piece of paper into a small ball. Wind some adhesive tape around it.

3. Tape a piece of string or yarn, about 30cm (12in) long, to the ball.

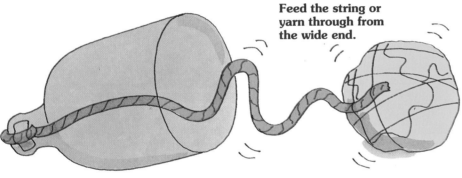

Feed the string or yarn through from the wide end.

4. Remove the bottle cap. Feed the string or yarn through the bottle and tape the end to the outside of the bottle neck, using adhesive tape.

5. Holding the bottle by its neck, see how many times you can toss the ball up into the air and then catch it in the cup-shaped opening in the bottle.

Scoop ball

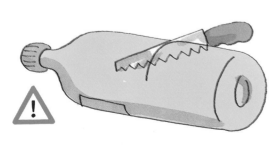

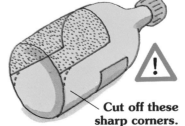

1. Cut a large plastic bottle so that it measures about 25cm (10in) from the neck.

2. Using scissors, cut out a section, as shown above. Round off the corners for safety.

Cut off these sharp corners.

3. Make a second scoop and use them to throw and catch a paper ball between two people.

Guessing box

Using an old shoe box, you can create an intriguing guessing game. To make sure that the game doesn't get boring, collect a good stock of things to use as mystery objects, with a variety of sizes, shapes and textures. Don't use sharp or prickly objects.

You will need
- Shoe box • Full food can
- Ruler • Felt-tip pen
- Kitchen cloth or some other light fabric
- Adhesive tape • Bread knife
- Scissors • Various small objects

Making the box

   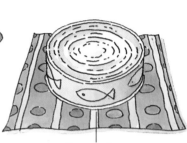

Cut up here.

1. Using a bread knife, carefully cut a large rectangle out of one of the small sides of a shoe box. Take care not to cut yourself.

2. Put a can over the middle of the opposite end. Draw around it, using a felt-tip pen. The shape will form the basis for another hole.

3. Make sure that you will be able to fit your hand inside the hole. Then push the end of the knife into the circle and cut it out carefully.

4. Using the can as a guide, cut a rectangle of fabric that will be large enough to cover the circle easily. Cut it in half up the middle.

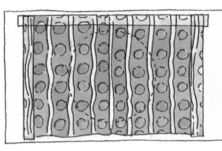

5. Tape along the top and down the sides of the fabric. Then tape the cloth to the inside of the box so that it covers the round hole. Replace the box lid. Make sure that you cannot see inside the box through the material covered hole.

Q. How do mice behave after they have argued?

A. They refuse to squeak to each other.

How to play

One person, the chooser, chooses a variety of small objects, keeping them out of sight of the guesser. The chooser puts one of the objects into the box through the rectangular hole. The guesser puts a hand through the fabric to feel the mystery object and tries to guess what it is.

Other ideas to try

Memory box

Put several objects inside the box and remove the lid so that the guesser can take a good look. Put the lid back on, then ask the guesser to look away. Remove one object and shuffle the remaining things around. Take the lid off again and see if the guesser can tell what is missing.

Tasting box

Put different foods on saucers. Then put one of the saucers inside the box. The guesser dips a wet finger into the saucer and tastes it without looking.

Secret messages

Sometimes spies have to send secret messages to each other. You could do this with your friends, using unusual writing materials such as potatoes and wax. To be really secretive, you could write your messages using a code. One code, called the Pigpen alphabet, is shown on the opposite page.

Q. Where do spies do their shopping?

A. At the snoop-ermarket.

Q. What do you call spies who will not say how old they are?

A. Secret age-ents.

Make a pen

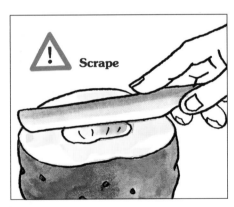

To make a pen that does not leave noticeable marks on paper, sharpen one end of a used match with a piece of sandpaper or a nail file.

Potato inkwell

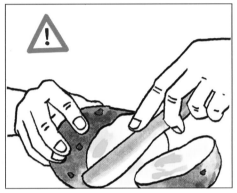

1. Hold the potato as shown here and cut off both ends with a table knife. Be sure to keep your fingers out of the way of the knife.

2. Stand the potato on one end. Scoop a hole in the top with a spoon.

3. Use the blade of the knife to scrape and squeeze the juice from the cut top of the potato into the hole that you scooped out of it.

Scrape

4. Dip the sharpened end of a used match into the potato ink to write the message. When the ink dries, the message will be invisible.

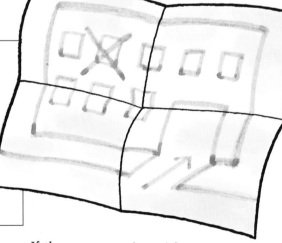

If the message is put in a warm oven it will emerge looking like this. You could make other inks out of lemon juice, milk, onion juice or cola.

Writing messages

When you write your secret messages, you'll need to include secret marks, which will be known only by you and your contact. When your contact reads your ordinary looking letter, the secret marks will show how to make a message appear on the paper. Examples of these secret marks are shown in the letter on the right.

WX stands for wax message, while X shows which side of the paper carries the message. You might like to make up your own secret marks.

RAINY DAY
SPYCATCHER'S CLUB
BOX WX 123

DEAR C,

MEET ME FOR DINNER AT 8.

WITH LOVE,
A

Code to indicate the secret writing method.

You can find out how to make this secret writing in the section below called "Pigpen code".

Code to show which side of the paper the secret writing is on.

Wax writing

Wax writing is simple to do. Use a white candle, or your message will not be invisible.

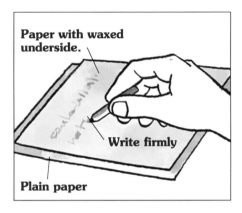

Paper with waxed underside.

Write firmly

Plain paper

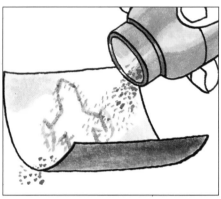

1. To begin, wax some thin paper by rubbing all over it with a white candle. Then lay the waxed side onto a piece of writing paper.

2. Press firmly to print your message on the paper. The person who receives the letter should sprinkle it with some coffee powder or chalk dust.

3. When he or she gives the paper a gentle shake, the powder will stick to the message and slide off the rest of the paper.

Pigpen code

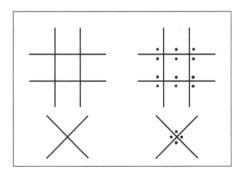

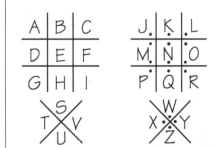

GERMANY

1. This mysterious-looking code is easy to use. To make the key, start by drawing the patterns that are shown in the picture above.

2. Now write the letters of the alphabet like this. The pattern of lines, or lines and dots next to each other, is used to stand for that letter.

3. This example shows how the word Germany looks in Pigpen code. Now see if you can decipher the message that is written on the letter.

More origami

Using origami techniques, you can make paper animals, such as the jumping frogs shown here. These have springy back legs, which make them leap into the air. You could hold a competition between several jumping frogs.

Q. What type of frog is useful to shipping?

A. A frog horn.

Smaller frogs are good for high jumps.

How to make your frogs

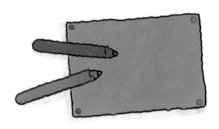

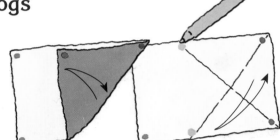

1. Label the corners of the paper red and blue as shown, on both sides. For the most eye-catching results, you could use paper that is decorated on one side only.

2. With the plain side facing you, fold a blue corner to touch the long side of the paper. Then unfold it.

3. Fold and unfold the other blue corner in the same way. Mark the ends of the new creases with yellow dots on both sides.

Double legs are more springy.

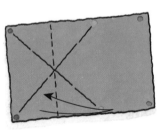

4. Turn the paper over. Fold the blue corners to the yellow marks. Unfold them. After unfolding, the paper should stick up slightly.

5. Put a finger at each end of the last crease and push it in gently.

6. If the creases are firm, the middle will pop up, bringing the blue marks towards the yellow ones.

Make a high jump

To make a high jump for your frog to hop over, use coins and a thin strip of cardboard for a bar. Every time your frog clears the bar, add a coin.

You can use a few techniques to make your frog jump higher. For example, you could bend the front and back legs back a second time. Also, you could make your frog using springy cardboard, as used for birthday cards.

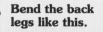

Bend the front legs like this.

Bend the back legs like this.

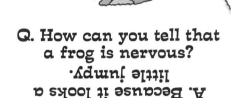

Q. What equipment does a frog use to repair things?

A. A toad's tool.

You could decorate your frogs with similar markings to a real frog.

You might like to decorate a frog with spots.

You might prefer to make your frogs look totally unrealistic, with garish stripes.

Q. How can you tell that a frog is nervous?

A. Because it looks a little jumpy.

This point forms the nose of the frog.

7. Flatten the blue corners beneath the yellow marks and turn the paper over.

8. Fold the blue corners up to the point. This will make the frog's front feet.

9. Find the edges between the dots. Fold them to meet in the middle.

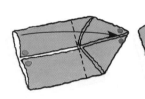 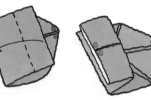 

10. Fold the red dotted side over the front feet so that only the front point sticks out.

11. Fold the edge with the red dots back again to meet the last fold that you made.

12. Turn your frog over. Pull the front feet down a little to make it stand straight.

You could draw on the eyes, using black felt-tip.

To make the frog jump, press down in the middle of its back at the edge of the paper. Allow your finger to slide off.

Target jumping

You could make a lily pond target and try to get your frog to jump into the middle of it. Cut a large blue paper circle for a pond. Draw on lots of lilies and write different scores on each one. See who has the most points after ten jumps.

Paperfold kite

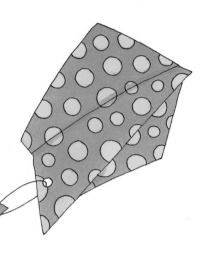

You can make simple kites from any type of thin paper. To make one that shimmers you could use silver wrapping paper, which you can buy from birthday card shops. Whatever you make your kite from, it will fly best in a very gentle breeze. For tips on how to fly it, turn to page 96.

For tips on how to fly it, turn to page 96.

You will need

- 3 pieces of thin paper 21 x 29.5cm (8½ x 11in)
- Thin drinking straw
- Clear adhesive tape
- Cotton thread
- Paper clip
- 10m (33ft) tough thread
- Lots of pieces of paper, to make a tail

Making the kite

When folding the kite, lay a ruler between the dots and fold the paper over it.

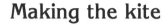

2cm (¾in)

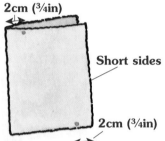

Short sides

2cm (¾in)

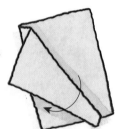

1. Take one of the pieces of paper. Fold the short sides to meet each other. At the very top, mark a dot 2cm (¾in) from the left corner. At the very bottom, mark a dot 2cm (¾in) from the right corner.

2. Pull the top layer in your direction and make a fold between the dots. Now turn the whole sheet of paper over. Fold the top piece over, so that the crease matches the one that is directly underneath.

3. Unfold the top piece of paper again, then turn the whole sheet over. Lay a ruler between the left and right corners and draw a pencil line across the paper, as shown in the picture above.

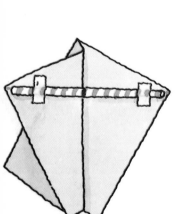

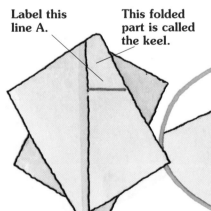

Label this line A.

This folded part is called the keel.

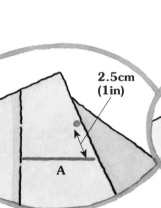

2.5cm (1in)

A

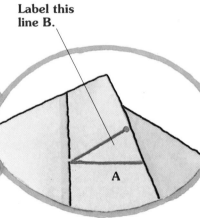

Label this line B.

A

4. Mark the middle of the straw. Lay it along the line with the mark on the kite's middle fold. Put adhesive tape on each side.

5. Turn the kite over. Lay a ruler between the left and right corners. Draw a line across the folded part only. Label it A.

6. Mark a dot on the folded edge, 2.5cm (1in) above line A. Then draw a line from the dot to where A meets the middle fold.

Making a reel and a kite line

To make a reel, fold another piece of paper in half four times, then in half lengthwise. Tie a 10m (33ft) length of thread around the reel. Wind it up.

Tie the other end of the thread securely to a paper clip. Push the paper clip firmly onto the kite at line A.

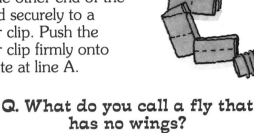

21cm (8¼in)

29.5cm (11½in)

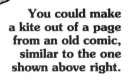

Q. What do you call a fly that has no wings?

A. A walk.

You could make a kite out of a page from an old comic, similar to the one shown above right.

Making the tail

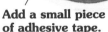

2cm (¾in)

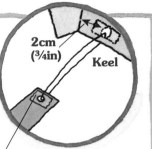

2cm (¾in)

Keel

Add a small piece of adhesive tape.

Cut the third piece of paper into long strips 2cm (¾in) wide. Decorate them vividly and glue them together to make a tail 80cm (31½in) long. Make a hole in one end with a pencil.

Make a hole near the bottom of the keel, 2cm (¾in) out from the kite's middle fold. Tie the tail on with a 30cm (12in) piece of thread. Add adhesive tape as shown above.

You could decorate a plain paper kite with a simple face.

Flight tests

When your kite is finished, test fly it with the paper clip attached in different places. If the wind is gentle it will probably fly best if you position the paper clip on line A. Try it on line B if the breeze is a little stronger.

Other ideas

To make your kites as visible as possible, you could make them using brightly decorated paper or design a pattern for yourself. On the right are a number of ideas for patterns. You could use these suggestions as the bases for your own style of decoration. For further inspiration, you might like to look at the markings of wild animals, such as tigers or exotic fish.

Stripes. These should make V shapes from the middle, as shown here.

Polka dots. For a loose effect, paint on your dots, using a large brush.

Dazzling stripes. Use thick felt-tip pens to make this effect.

Zebra stripes. Copy the appearance of a zebra by drawing bold, black, swirling stripes on your kite.

Q. Why did the man tie his watch to his kite?

A. Because he wanted to make time fly.

Code machines

Code machines are useful for encoding and decoding messages quickly. You could use them to make up codes to use in invisible messages, like those shown on pages 82-83. The easiest ones to make are shown below and are in the form of strips. Code wheels (shown on the next page) are harder to make, but they are more fun to use.

Q. What do you call a secret agent with eight legs?

A. A spy-der.

Code strips

1. For the coded strip, start by drawing 52 equal-sized boxes, about 0.5 x 1cm (¼ x ½in). Cut the boxes into a long strip. Putting a letter in each box, write out the complete alphabet twice.

2. Next, make a strip that contains 26 boxes. In it, write out the alphabet once. To make a code, place the shorter strip anywhere along the longer strip, so that the letters are next to letters on the longer strip.

As an example, place your shorter strip so that A is next to G on the long strip. In your message, every A you write should be replaced by G. Similarly, every B will be replaced by H, and so on. Call this code "Code G".

Plain alphabet strip

| A | B | C | D | E | F | G | H | I | J | K | L | M | N | O | P | Q | R | S | T | U | V | W | X | Y | Z |

| A | B | C | D | E | F | G | H | I | J | K | L | M | N | O | P | Q | R | S | T | U | V | W | X | Y | Z | A | B | C | D | E | F | G | H | I | J | K | L | M | N | O | P | Q | R | S | T | U | V | W | X | Y | Z |

Coded strip, containing two alphabets.

Here, the start of the top strip is lined up with the letter G on the bottom strip. This creates the Code G alphabet, to be read from the bottom strip.

The message on the right is written in Code T. To work it out (and reveal more details of how to disguise your messages cunningly) match A on your plain alphabet strip with T on the coded strip.

When you send messages, be sure to let your receivers know which code alphabet you have used, so that they can decode your message. You should also make sure that they have code machines of their own, or they will not be able to translate your message.

FTDX VHWXL MKBVDR MH VKTVD UR UKXTDBGZ PHK WLBG HW WIET VXL.

Code wheel pattern

On the finished machine, turn the inner wheel to reveal the code. For example, for Code G, turn this wheel until A is next to G on the outer wheel.

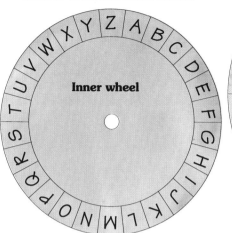

Inner wheel

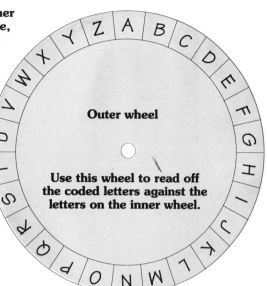

Outer wheel

Use this wheel to read off the coded letters against the letters on the inner wheel.

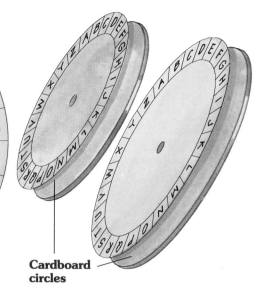

Cardboard circles

1. To make a code wheel, trace both of the above patterns carefully onto two separate pieces of stiff paper.*

2. Print a letter in each of the spaces in the circles. When you have done the same for both wheels, cut both of them out.

3. To make the wheels harder wearing, fix them to circles of cardboard (cut from cereal boxes, for instance).

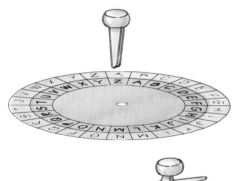

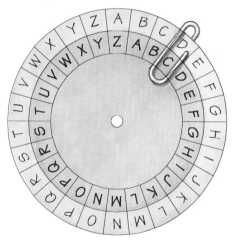

4. Push a paper fastener through both middle dots. Twist it once to make a round hole. Bend out the tabs.

Alternatively, press a thumb tack through the middle of both wheels and into a small pencil eraser or a piece of wood.

5. Use a paper clip to hold the wheels in place when you have matched the plain alphabet with a code alphabet.

Double codes

1. To make a double code, first write your message and then choose the codes you will use, such as T and S.

2. Print the names of the two codes over every other letter, so that you will know how to encode it, as shown below.

3. Set your code strip or wheel for the first code and encode all the letters marked with that letter, as shown here.

4. Set the strip at the second code and encode all the remaining letters. Combine the codes for your final code.

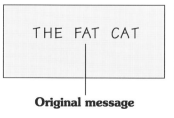

Original message

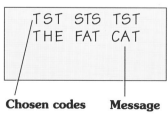

Chosen codes   Message

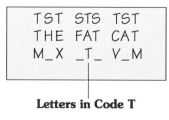

Letters in Code T

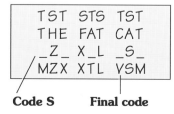

Code S   Final code

*For details about tracing see page 93.

Flying squirrel

Flying squirrels are found in North and South America. They can glide from tree to tree. They have stretched skin between their front and back legs, like wings, and bushy tails, which they use for balance. To make this flying model start by copying the template on page 95.

copying the template on page 95.

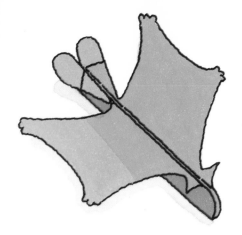

You will need
- Stiff paper 20cm x 22cm (8in x 8½in)
- Ball-point pen
- Adhesive tape
- Model dough
- Ruler • Scissors
- Felt-tip pens

Q. What happens if a flying squirrel forgets how to fly?

A. It gets in a flap.

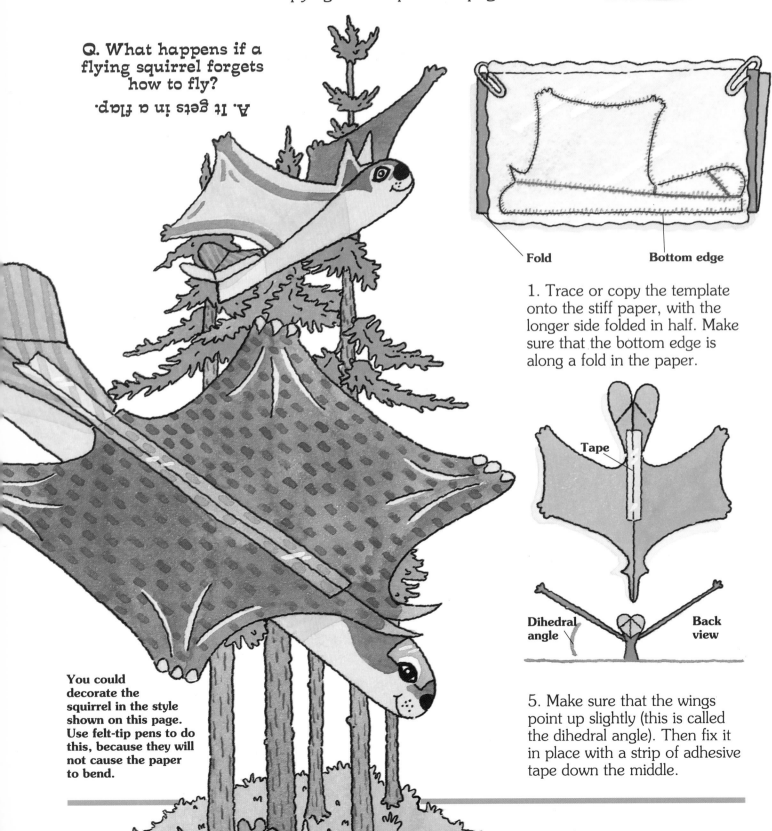

Fold   **Bottom edge**

1. Trace or copy the template onto the stiff paper, with the longer side folded in half. Make sure that the bottom edge is along a fold in the paper.

Tape

Dihedral angle   **Back view**

5. Make sure that the wings point up slightly (this is called the dihedral angle). Then fix it in place with a strip of adhesive tape down the middle.

You could decorate the squirrel in the style shown on this page. Use felt-tip pens to do this, because they will not cause the paper to bend.

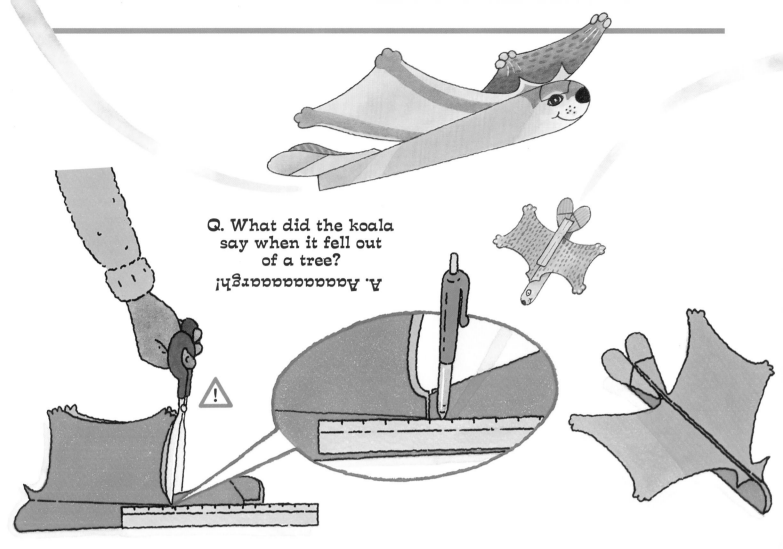

Q. What did the koala say when it fell out of a tree?

A. Aaaaaaaaargh!

2. Cut along the red lines using a pair of scissors, to make sure that the cuts are crisp and straight. The cuts will separate the wings from the tail.

3. Next, score along the blue lines using a ball-point pen. The pen will press into the stiff paper, creating a crease which you can fold easily.

4. Bend the wings and tail out along the score lines. Don't bend them out too far or they will droop down, making the squirrel hard to fly.

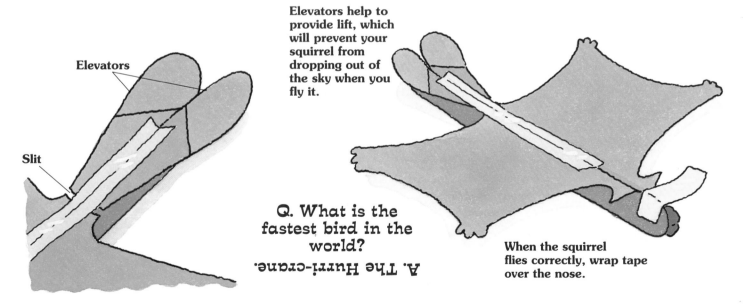

Elevators

Slit

Elevators help to provide lift, which will prevent your squirrel from dropping out of the sky when you fly it.

Q. What is the fastest bird in the world?

A. The Hurri-crane.

When the squirrel flies correctly, wrap tape over the nose.

6. When you put the tape on, make sure that the wings and tail are held at different angles. The tail should point up slightly at the slit.

7. For stability, make elevators by bending the ends of the tail up slightly along the score lines, as shown in the two pictures above.

8. Put model dough inside the nose to add weight. If the squirrel dives, bend the elevators up more. If it stalls, remove some model dough.

Kaleidoscope

Kaleidoscopes make fascinating, ever-changing patterns. To make one you can use mirror board, which you can buy from art shops, or you can use cooking foil instead, stuck to a piece of cardboard.

You will need
- Mirror board (or cardboard covered in cooking foil) 15 x 15cm (6 x 6in)
- 1 sheet of wrapping paper
- Tracing paper
- 1 sheet of thin, clear plastic
- Bright, patterned paper, cut into tiny shapes
- Adhesive tape • Glue
- Felt-tip pen
- Pencil • Ruler • Scissors

The mirrors should face one another.

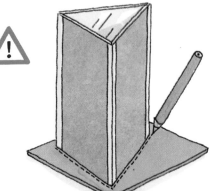

1. First, cut the mirror board into three strips of equal width. Then tape the long sides of the mirrors together.

2. Stand the triangular tube you have made on some cardboard. Draw around its shape and then cut it out using scissors.

3. Tape the cut-out cardboard to the mirrors. When it is in place, push a sharp pencil into the middle to make a hole.

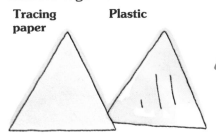

Tracing paper   **Plastic**

4. Place the triangular tube on the sheets of plastic and tracing paper. Draw around the tube and then cut out the shapes.

5. Tape the plastic and tracing paper triangles together, along two of their three sides. This will create a kind of pocket.

6. Put the bright pieces of paper into the pocket, then seal up the third side. Finally, tape the pocket to the open end of the tube, making sure that the tracing paper goes on the outside. Then point the end containing the paper bits to the light and look through the tiny hole.

Q. What do you call a mirror that can do magic?

A. A mirror-cle.

The mirrors reflect the shapes in a pretty pattern, which changes when you shake the kaleidoscope.

Templates

Bat (page 24)

Trace this shape onto tracing paper, then lay the tracing so that the straight line lies along the folded edge of some thin cardboard. On your tracing, make sure that you show the lines that are printed here in red and blue.

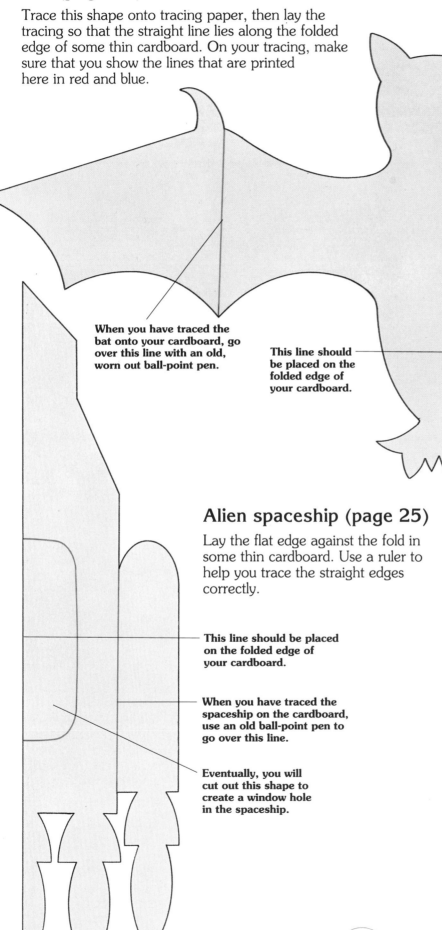

When you have traced the bat onto your cardboard, go over this line with an old, worn out ball-point pen.

This line should be placed on the folded edge of your cardboard.

Alien spaceship (page 25)

Lay the flat edge against the fold in some thin cardboard. Use a ruler to help you trace the straight edges correctly.

This line should be placed on the folded edge of your cardboard.

When you have traced the spaceship on the cardboard, use an old ball-point pen to go over this line.

Eventually, you will cut out this shape to create a window hole in the spaceship.

Tracing a template

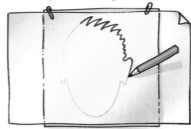

1. Lay some tracing paper over the template. Using paper clips, attach the tracing paper to the template. Trace the outline with a pencil.

2. Unclip the tracing and turn it over. Draw over the outline with a soft pencil, making sure that it is covered thickly. Turn the tracing over again.

3. Lay the tracing on top of some paper or cardboard. Pressing fairly hard with a pencil or ball-point pen, scribble over the tracing, so that a line appears on the surface beneath.

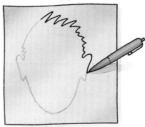

4. Remove the tracing paper. You should be able to see the tracing that has transferred onto the new surface. To make it more visible, go over the lines with a pencil or a ball-point pen.

Animal ears templates (pages 52-53)

Mouse ears

For these ears, the larger shapes will become the outsides of the ears. The smaller shapes, on the right, will become the insides of the ears. You will need to cut out two of each shape.

Usually, wild mice have ears that are pink and brown. If you want you could make your ears white, like a pet mouse.

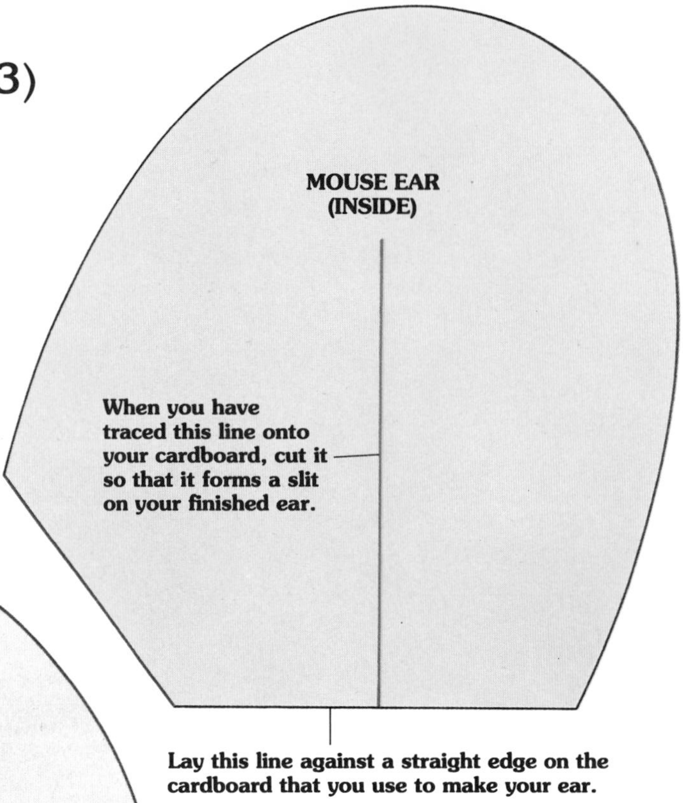

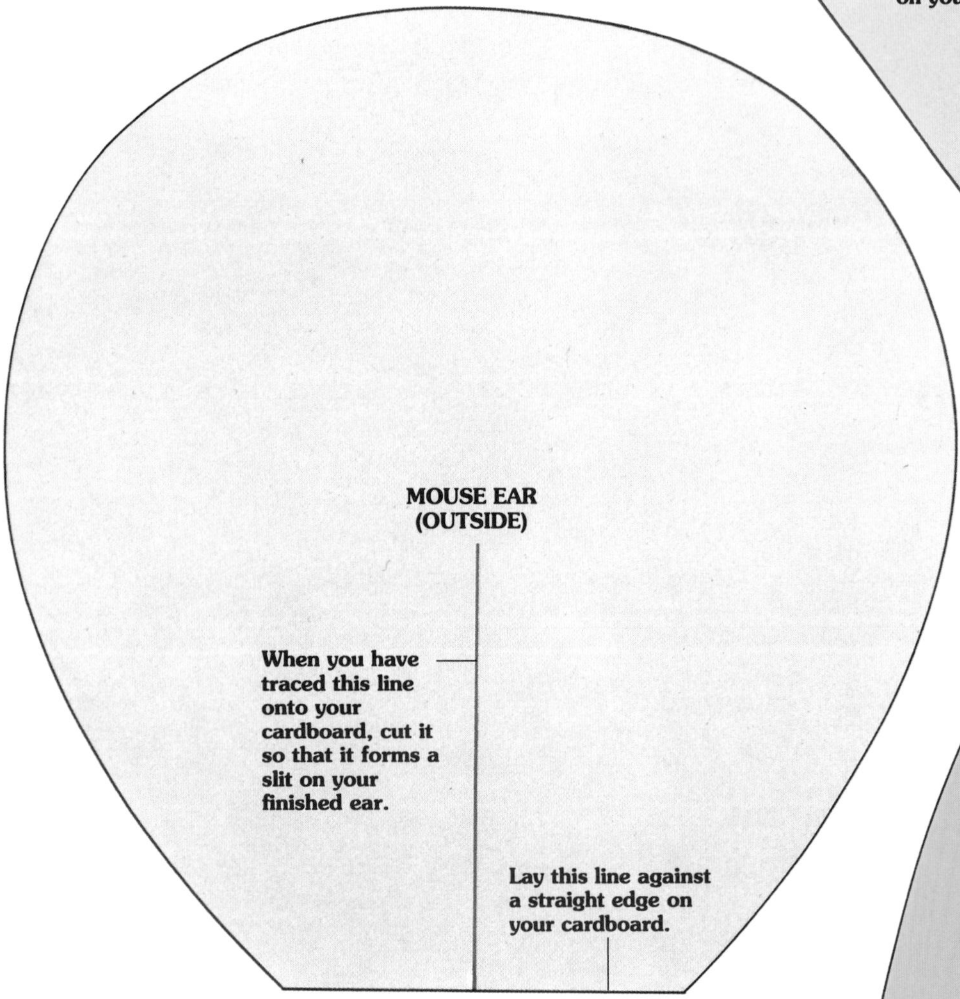

MOUSE EAR (INSIDE)

When you have traced this line onto your cardboard, cut it so that it forms a slit on your finished ear.

Lay this line against a straight edge on the cardboard that you use to make your ear.

MOUSE EAR (OUTSIDE)

When you have traced this line onto your cardboard, cut it so that it forms a slit on your finished ear.

Lay this line against a straight edge on your cardboard.

Cat ears

These cat ears are simpler to make than the mouse ears, because you do not have to make inner parts for them. This shape is shown in orange, suggesting that they are for a ginger cat. You could make your ears in any shade you like.

You could also use this template to make a pig's ears, using pink cardboard.

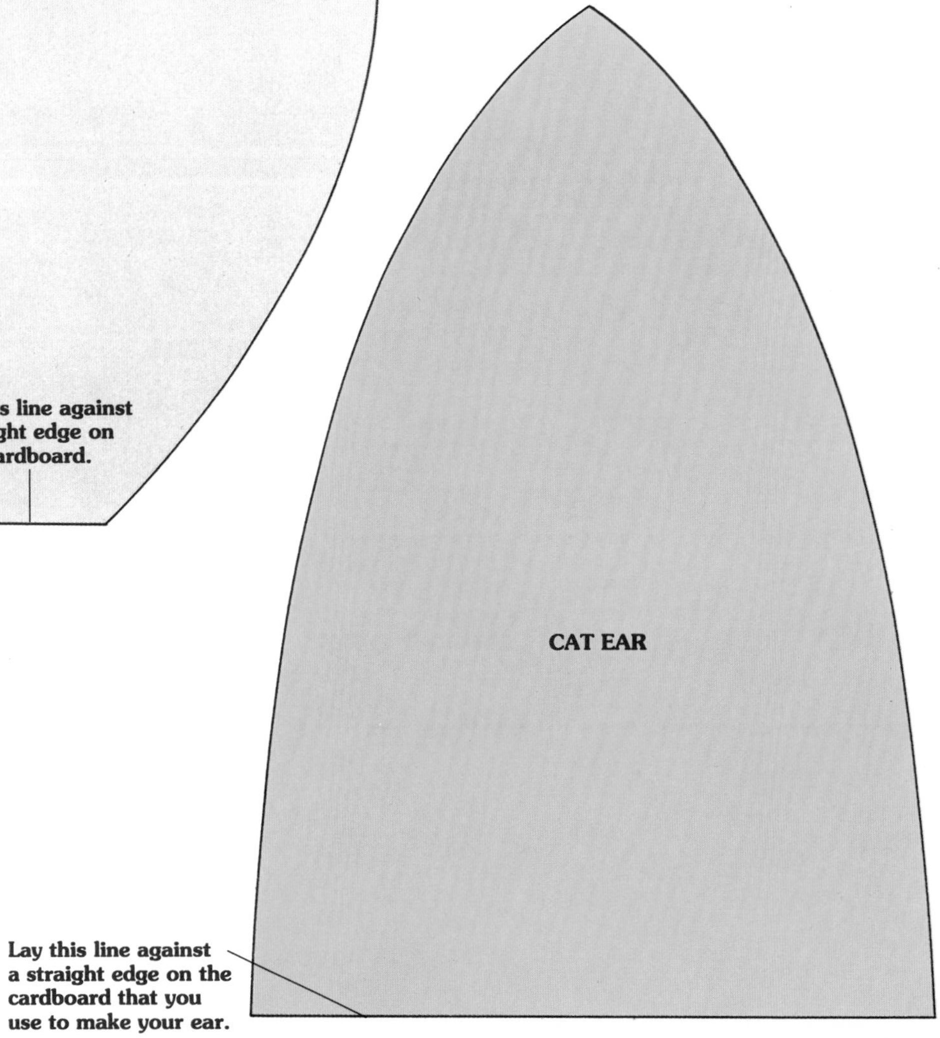

CAT EAR

Lay this line against a straight edge on the cardboard that you use to make your ear.

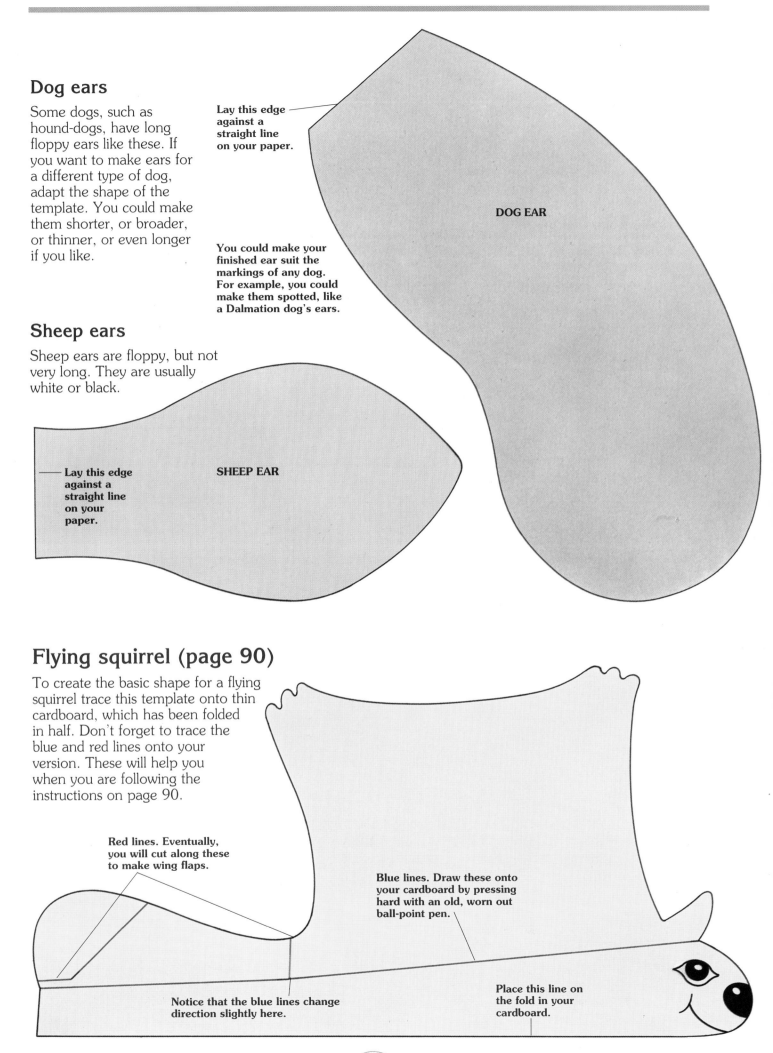

Dog ears

Some dogs, such as hound-dogs, have long floppy ears like these. If you want to make ears for a different type of dog, adapt the shape of the template. You could make them shorter, or broader, or thinner, or even longer if you like.

Lay this edge against a straight line on your paper.

You could make your finished ear suit the markings of any dog. For example, you could make them spotted, like a Dalmation dog's ears.

DOG EAR

Sheep ears

Sheep ears are floppy, but not very long. They are usually white or black.

Lay this edge against a straight line on your paper.

SHEEP EAR

Flying squirrel (page 90)

To create the basic shape for a flying squirrel trace this template onto thin cardboard, which has been folded in half. Don't forget to trace the blue and red lines onto your version. These will help you when you are following the instructions on page 90.

Red lines. Eventually, you will cut along these to make wing flaps.

Blue lines. Draw these onto your cardboard by pressing hard with an old, worn out ball-point pen.

Notice that the blue lines change direction slightly here.

Place this line on the fold in your cardboard.

Test results and kite tips

Density tests (pages 64-65)

This chart shows the results for the density tests. All of the tests were made when the liquids were the same temperature. If your liquids are different temperatures when you do the tests, your results might be different from those shown here.

LIQUID	RESULT
FRUIT CORDIAL, TREACLE, MAPLE SYRUP	THESE SINK. THIS MEANS THAT THEY ARE DENSER THAN WATER.
COOKING OIL	THIS FLOATS. IT IS LESS DENSE THAN WATER.
MILK, ORANGE JUICE	THESE MIX WITH WATER. THIS MEANS THAT THEY HAVE MORE OR LESS THE SAME DENSITY AS WATER.

Flying a kite (pages 86-87)

When the weather is good, you will probably want to take your paper kite out to fly it. Wherever you go to fly it, take a friend to help you. It's more fun than going alone.

Where to fly

The best places to fly a kite are open spaces such as fields and uncrowded beaches. Before you go, check with a grown-up that kite flying is not forbidden in the place you want to visit.

Flying tips

- The best conditions for flying are in moderate winds. If the wind is too strong or too weak, wait for better kite-flying weather.
- Take some adhesive tape with you. If your kite gets damaged, you can use it to make some on-the-spot repairs.
- Wear gloves to stop the kite line from cutting into your hands.
- Don't fly your kite near roads.
- Don't fly your kite near overhead cables.
- To avoid being struck by lightning, don't fly your kite in a thunderstorm.

Launching a kite

1. Check that all the knots on your kite are secure before you launch it. If they are not tight the kite might break loose and blow away.

2. Stand with your back to the wind. Then get your helper to hold the kite up as shown on the right. Let out about 5m (16ft) of line.

3. Tell your helper to push the kite up into the air. Try not to tug at the kite, or the line might snap.

4. Slowly let out more line. If the kite starts to fall, pull the line gently. As it rises again, let out more line.

Flying alone

Stand with the wind behind you. Hold the kite by its towing point, so that it faces into the wind. Let out a little line with the other hand. Release the kite gently into the air. As the wind lifts the kite, steadily let out more of the line.

Bringing down the kite

Bring down your kite carefully. To do this, wind the line slowly around the reel, or ask your helper to pull the line down for you, while you wind it up. Make sure that you don't tug the line too sharply, or the line might snap.